PRAISE FOR
SEVEN DOORS Of THE FIREMAKER

Marina Walker has given us an engrossing tale of discovery and transformation. Unfolding like the heroic journey described by Joseph Campbell, The Firemaker takes us into remarkable experiences. Here, in a vivid fable, is a guide to the possibilities of the spiritual path.

—Jonathan Young, Ph.D. Psychology
Founding Curator, *Joseph Campbell Archives*

Seven Doors Of The Firemaker is a deceptively easy read about the most complex of subjects, the intertwining of the human psyche and spirit. Marina Walker has created more than a novel here. This is a traveler's guide to personal transformation.

—J. Michael Ross
Author of *The MotherSong* and *Goddy*

Dr. Walker's character, Helen, is the essence of the fragile and injured spirit of humankind. Through her journey we learn how the power of insight, resilience, and self-discovery can help us to achieve joy and wholeness.

—Jo-Anne Blatter, LCSW
Creator of *The Aphrodite Project*, Documentary Film
Official Selection, Santa Barbara Film Festival—2004

SEVEN DOORS
Of
THE FIREMAKER

A Novel

Marina R. Walker

SEVEN DOORS
Of
THE FIREMAKER

Marina R. Walker

OakStar Press

New York - 2005

This book is a work of fiction.
All events, locations, people and incidents are fictitious.
Any resemblance to real persons living or dead,
or actual events or places is purely coincidental.

OakStar Press
1133 Broadway, Suite 706
New York, NY 10010
www.OakStarPress.com

Library of Congress Cataloging-in-Publishing Data
(Provided by Quality Books, Inc.)

Walker, Marina R.
Seven doors of the firemaker/ Marina R. Walker

p.   cm.
ISBN 0-9762674-0-3

1.   Spiritual life—Fiction. 2. Metaphysics—Fiction.
2.   Success—Fiction. 4. Adventure stories. I. Title.

PS 3623.A3596S48 2005 813'.6
QBI04-700550

First Printing September 2005

10 9 8 7 6 5 4 3 2 1

Cover Art adapted from *Cycles Gladiator*
G. Massias Print, Circa 1900—Artist Unknown
Author's Cover Photo—Dave Palmer

Printed in the USA

For the One who showed me The Doors

For Michael, who gave me a new life

For Ashleigh, my girl, who showed me how to love Helen

And for Henry, who helped me come down off the shelf

ACKNOWLEDGMENTS

Wes, whose big heart gave me a place to rest; Gordy, whose devoted friendship supported the visible and invisible patterns of my wholeness; Lyndsay, who encouraged the magic to come out; Shawn, for his truth and tireless *flametending*; Allen, whose steady presence was a safe harbor through many storms; Eileen, whose focused compassion taught me how to nourish myself; Allan, whose generosity and kindness showed me what had been missing; Walter, for teaching Helen how to sail; Diadre, for her love; and Sri whose clarity revealed the final key.

For their special editorial and other contributions to my manuscript, many thanks to Lainey Emoto and Gordon Coburn.

To all the other Allies and Angels whose care, wisdom, grace and companionship helped me forward on my journey, and to all who came for solace and stayed to grow, your willingness and courage expand my humanity.

Most beginnings are small, and appear trivial and insignificant, but in reality they are the most important things in life.

— James Allen

PROLOGUE

(Dear reader…please don't skip this part!)

One way to find the missing piece you're looking for — and I know you're looking for it — is to get on and off the bus that Virgie drives. Then, a day later, you ride your old yellow Huffy bike down the hill toward the garden and into, well, you'll see.

If you decide to go this route, the garden's in the back, behind Peri's house, which sits on the banks of the Little Dreamy. Watch out for the cats.

For me, it wasn't all that far to Peri's House and the rest. Well…yes it was. In truth, I guess it was both near *and* far.

I wouldn't have said this before my journey in the Land Behind the Doors, but now I know that often those words, *near and far*, are just abstractions, fuzzy doodles in the head without any firm mooring in reality. Tug on them just a little, and they shift.

More times than not, *near* sits facing the back of *far* on the Ring of Life like a couple of people riding tandem on a bicycle.

Far is just us expecting that what we desire could only exist somewhere a long way off. *Far* is just us bending our sight all the way around the Ring of Life and right back to *near*, where what we wanted had been sitting right next to us all the time.

What's *that* mean? It means that sometimes if we'd simply *turn around* we'd find ourselves already standing within arm's reach of our destination.

It's shocking to realize that we can be living in separate realities simultaneously, each reality at loggerheads with the other.

We might be outwardly steeling ourselves for some epic journey that stretches out far ahead—a quest to finally reach that elusive goal of *inner peace and power*. But at the same time we may secretly believe at the center of our being that there is absolutely no way for us to ever get there at all.

Often, that is when Life unexpectedly intervenes, keeping us on track in spite of our split realities. The next thing we know, we turn around and bang! There it is! Right next to us, hiding in plain sight where it has been all along.

It's a tricky place, the Ring of Life, lots of smoke and mirrors. Lots of illusions, misdirection, and shifting sand beneath the feet. It can make it look as if *nothing* but an epic journey will get us there. And sometimes that's true. But not always.

Don't get me wrong, an epic journey can be compelling and infinitely interesting and I'm about to share *my* epic journey with you. Obviously I believe it's important or I wouldn't be doing this.

The trouble with an epic journey, though, is that it's always so darned much work. But I happen to think that once you hear my story, you just might be empowered to save yourself some very intense *far*, turn around, and jump right into the *near* that holds what you're looking for.

That could mean skipping a lot of the lost time you would have to invest if you went it alone, not to mention the drama.

Here's the thing: I know that no matter *who you are*, the First Door is always *near*, waiting for you to enter. Regardless of appearances, this has always been true. Just as it's true that the help that comes along with going through that door is waiting for you, too.

Even if it *feels* as if you're all messed up, even if you've been feeling that way for years and years, you can enter and help will be there to guide you. It might be anybody or anything.

It might be a waitress, a beekeeper, or a frog, but somebody or something will be there to help you if you will make that first leap of faith.

I'm living proof. You can go in that First Door with blurry vision, a broken heart and no idea what you're doing. And you can come back out of the Last Door absolutely whole with light in your eyes and fire in your heart.

When that happens, things you've never known will be known. Creative possibilities you've never dared hope for will burst out like spring flowers. And those invisible but nasty traps you keep stepping into that hurt you so badly will stand out like one of those giant red, light-up noses that circus clowns wear.

Even more important, there's a very good chance you'll discover that being intuitive and aware does *not* require you to walk around with a long, serious face. And being courageous doesn't mean you have to lose your joy or develop a hide as thick as leather. But you'll see what I mean by all that later.

Now let me tell you about my adventure...

CHAPTER 1

THE MIRACLE OF PLASTIC AND BANANAS

Remember Alice? In Wonderland, I mean. Right. That one. Well, if you ask Alice, or me for that matter, we'd both have to say it's amazing how fast you can get sucked down a rabbit hole and into the adventure of a lifetime.

That's exactly what happened to both of us, except *my* rabbit hole turned out to be a seat on a bus right behind Virgie Washington, city bus driver. I didn't know it at the time, but when I got off at my stop, less than ten minutes after meeting her, the rabbit hole had me. And when my journey was over, my life was changed forever.

It started like this…

Following some strategic problems with gravity and the weather that required a little help from Virgie, I finally got on the bus after waiting for about twenty minutes at a stop just off the freeway. You know the kind, just a sign with a picture of a bus and a bench with no shelter over it. Zero help when it's raining buckets, and it was.

By the time Virgie pulled up, the rain had worked its magic and the bottom of my overstuffed brown paper bag had just turned to oatmeal. She eased the bus to a stop and opened the door.

In keeping with several of the major laws of physics, my little stash of groceries, tuna sandwich and bottle of Diet Coke, all met the sidewalk at precisely the same time, then headed off in as many directions as they could manage to head off into.

Up to that point, my whole life had been a lot like that. Rain coming down, bottom falling out. You get it, a tapestry of wars and flowers, and yawns.

Unfortunately, there had been many more wars than flowers, and the yawns, of varying lengths and intensities, dotted my landscape like wildly proliferating weeds.

Actually, right at that moment, my life resembled an extended yawn, but that didn't mean there wasn't pain, too. There was, and lots of it.

I don't intend to spend much time on the pain at this point because either you've experienced it for yourself or you know someone who has. My backstory is pretty simple really, and I'll get into it later.

The main thing to know about all of that right now is that if you grow up in a family that hits instead of hugs, screams instead of talks, and breaks dishes against the wall instead of mending wounds, you end up with a kind of primal ache that never goes away.

It becomes systemic. It's as if there's this disgruntled organ called *pain* that doesn't work right, or maybe it works too well. And it's sitting there inside you right next to your spleen, stomach, lungs, and the rest of it.

In my case, I made my break from all that as a teenager on a Sunday afternoon while my parents were busy barking at each other over something.

It was always something that somebody, probably my mother, had done, or not done, or should have done better. Anyway, they were deep into their personal combat zone, and I knew it was time for me to bail out.

It was such a nonevent, in a way. No drama. Just a little tip of my imaginary hat to a set of parents who didn't notice I was leaving anyway. I simply walked out the front door of the house that day and never looked back. My farewell note read:

> **Dear Carl and Val,**
>
> **Checking out permanently.**
> **Go ahead and rent my room.**
>
> **Adios,**
> **Helen**

It wasn't very eloquent, I admit, and very light on gratitude. After all, they clothed, fed and housed me. But I was a teenager who was pretty light on the Big Picture back then, you know?

Anyway, the point is that leaving home probably saved my life. It most certainly saved my sanity. But it didn't stop the pain.

Something else was going to have to do that and so far, at least up to the moment I met Virgie, whatever that *something* was remained as elusive as a winning lottery ticket.

Men didn't do it and work didn't do it. Hauling my buns to a new place to live didn't do it. Food didn't do it. Alcohol and pills didn't do it.

Those were all the big and little wars I'd fought and survived during the ten years since I pulled my jail break from home, and the only thing I knew for sure was—they didn't do it.

"I'm sorry I can't help you with all that mess there, honey," Virgie said, "but if I get out of the bus and somebody sees me, they'll have my hide back at the bus barn."

As she spoke, the rain decided to let up and turn itself into a light mist, thank God, making things a little more bearable as I gathered up my stuff.

"I've got this plastic bag here if you want to round all your things up in it," Virgie said, leaning down and handing me the bag. "Take your time. Nobody on here but me today and I'm about seven minutes ahead of schedule."

"Thanks. I really appreciate it." I even managed a little smile for her as I knelt there, my hair limp as spaghetti, glancing up at Virgie between scoops of stuff.

"Story of my life," I said, almost more to myself than to her. "The bottom is always falling out of something around me."

Virgie nodded and smiled while I herded the debris into a pile. "Everything's always falling apart, huh? I hear ya, darlin'. I know all about it. You got all your stuff there, now?"

I picked up the last of it, a squashed tomato and soggy notebook, looked around and decided that was all.

"Yeah, I think that's it."

4

"What's your stop?"

"Oak Street."

"Oak. Got it."

Virgie shoved a plump hand into a big blue backpack beside her seat and yanked out a small hand towel and another plastic shopping bag, then dove back in for something else. Patting the space on the seat behind her, she held out the towel, the plastic bag and a banana.

"Here you go. Come sit here behind Old Virgie. We'll get you dry, fed and where you're going. You can use this other bag for a rain hat if it's coming down when you get off. What's your name?"

I plopped down on the seat, slowly dried my face and hands, then began peeling the banana.

"Helen. Helen Brower."

Virgie peeled a banana for herself then eased the bus onto the freeway. "That's a pretty name — Helen. It's an old fashioned name. I like it."

I smiled, thanked her, sighed, looked out the window, and took a big bite of the banana.

Virgie looked at me in the rear view mirror. "Plastic sure is a miracle, isn't it?"

I considered that for a second, realizing I'd never thought of plastic as anything at all really, much less a miracle. But, of course, it is, when you stop to think about it.

Even though it has its downsides, there are a lot of miraculous things you can do with plastic, that's for sure. Like keep your stuff dry in the rain.

Just then a thought flashed through my head, as if someone were piping it in from a remote sound booth: "What *other* miracles are you ignoring in your life, Helen?"

5

It startled me because, along with that thought, the rain had stopped completely and there was a break in the clouds. Sunlight shot through in shafts and the day brightened beautifully.

"That's a miracle right there that I usually ignore," I thought. But before long, I was focused on all my problems again.

Virgie and I rode in silence for about five or six minutes, then she spoke. "You want to talk about it, honey?"

"Pardon?"

"Do you want to talk about it?"

"About what?" I asked.

"About you looking flat worn out and me imagining that it's got nothing to do with this rain and your bag falling apart. Am I right?"

"Oh, I'm okay. Things could be a whole lot worse, you know? If this is as bad as it gets...."

"Excuse me for interruptin', honey, but sounds to me like you're quotin' not *talkin.'* Talk to me."

I had to laugh. If Virgie hadn't stopped me, I might have rambled on for another ten minutes with my pathetic little clichés.

"You're right, Virgie, that's *not* how I feel. The real truth is that I'm worn out and I need a job and I don't even have a single lead and, well, you get it."

"Nothin' seems to be workin' out right, huh?"

"Exactly. Makes me nuts."

"What do you think would fix that?"

"Boy, don't I wish I knew. At this point, just a little work would be a huge breakthrough. At least that would help put out the financial fires, if not all the rest of them."

"Maybe what you need is *more* fire, not less."

"Sorry?"

Virgie smiled, "Oh, nothing honey. You said Oak was your stop, right? It's up next." She began to slow the bus and ease it toward the bus stop.

"Gosh, thanks for keeping track. I'd have completely missed it." I got up, quickly gathered my things, then walked up next to Virgie and waited for the bus to stop.

"Thanks for everything, Virgie, especially for the banana. That really hit the spot."

Virgie gave me a broad grin, followed by a serious look, one of those looks that seem to pierce right into your soul. Then she smiled again.

"A banana sure is a miracle, isn't it? It's even better than plastic. I'm sorry we didn't get to talk longer, Helen, but here, take this."

She reached into her breast pocket and pulled out a little notepad, clicked her ballpoint pen and wrote something down.

"It's gonna be okay, honey. You go home and dry out. Have a good sleep and call this nice lady in the morning. She's got what you're looking for."

I took the paper and glanced down at it but didn't read it. "What I'm looking for? I don't know what you mean, Virgie. Oh, work? Really?"

Virgie chuckled. "Oh, it'll be work all right, various kinds, too, but good work. You can count on that. Just call her. She's good people."

She reached for the lever and opened the door. "Don't mess up, now. You call that number tomorrow and go see this woman, hear? She'll fix you up."

She patted me on the arm as I placed my hand on the rail and headed off the bus.

As I stepped down, I looked at the paper and saw the name "Peri" and a phone number. I wasn't at all sure what she was sending me into, but my instincts told me that Virgie was all right, so wherever she was sending me would be all right, too.

"Thank you, Virgie," I said.

At the bottom of the steps I stopped and turned to face her and that's when the rabbit hole snatched me for sure.

For just for a split second, there was a flash of sunlight off a gold band on the middle finger of Virgie's right hand. And the sunlight seemed to light up what looked like a bright red silk gown with a hood that covered her head and hid her face in shadow.

It startled me for a second, but when I blinked, there was Virgie the bus driver smiling down at me, same as before. I'm sure my face was an astonished stare, but before I could say anything, Virgie smiled and spoke.

"Don't worry, Helen," she said, tapping her heart and then her head. "Pretty soon, you'll know." Then she closed the door, waved and pulled off down the street.

CHAPTER 2

PERSEPHONE'S CATS

The next morning after breakfast I made the call. The woman at the other end of Virgie's mysterious phone number sounded a bit quirky, but she was pleasant and lively enough to talk to.

The work was some kind of gardening job and even though it was still winter, in this part of the country winters are typically so mild that gardening goes on pretty much year round.

And I love plants and had done a bit of gardening before. So I figured, what the heck, maybe she'd hire me. She gave me her address and off I went.

I peddled my yellow bicycle up a considerable hill toward the address she'd given me, thinking all the time, as I always did, about my problems. I hoped this job, since any other prospects fell under the category "None," would bring in enough cash to

9

tide me over until I could sort things out and find something more substantial.

Not a bad idea, on paper anyway. But in reality I'd only been trying to "sort things out" my entire life. I had to chuckle at my never-ending folly, even in the middle of gasping for breath.

With a big gulp of air, I yanked up the zipper of my blue windbreaker and reached down deep for one last burst of energy to make my way over the crest of the hill. I topped out and relaxed as I began the long coast to the bottom.

A few minutes later, I pulled up in front of an old Victorian house with a front door and trim the color of a ripe pomegranate, double checked the address, and locked my bike to a weathered YIELD sign.

There was no answer when I knocked on the front door. I waited a couple of minutes and tried again. This time, the door slowly swung open on its hinges.

Just then, there were scuffling noises and a loud thud as three or four cats shot out the door. I hesitated a moment, then cautiously pushed the door open the rest of the way. I stepped in, wondering if the woman I'd spoken to on the phone needed any help. From the sound of her voice, she was no kid.

"Hello? Anybody here?"

The room opened long and wide with arched ceilings and gleaming floors blanketed with patterned rugs faded by the sun and years of wear. They were clustered at angles and overlapped, forming a kind of haphazard meeting ground that led the eye to the centerpiece of the room, an enormous stone hearth where a cheery fire blazed.

Suddenly, I felt something brush by my shoulder. I turned to see a bright yellow, peach-faced lovebird flitting to safety on a nearby perch, high above a fat, yellow-eyed cat that came lumbering after her. Not nearly quick enough, the old cat, fat tail twitching, parked itself on a big green velvet sofa.

The bird chattered and ranted, mocking and scolding the cat. Head cocked, feathers fluffed, it took full advantage of being too high to suffer from any serious cat trouble.

I looked around and saw that there were a few more lovebirds roosting here and there as well as canaries, a couple of parrots, some finches and some other birds I didn't recognize.

A woman's voice rang out from the hallway, "Damn you, Elizabeth! Damn you, Eloise! You two stop snipping at each other!"

Just then, a spry, elderly woman with bottle-dyed red hair burst into the room waving a frazzled old broom. Elizabeth squawked once or twice and settled into preening her feathers.

Now the woman spotted me. "Holy moly, who the...?" She let her question trail off but kept the old broom cocked over her shoulder at the ready.

I quickly backed up a couple of steps. "Whoa! Hang on! Hang on! I'm Helen. I called about the gardening job?"

"Goodness sakes!"

The old woman quickly lowered her weapon and chuckled. "Of course you're Helen! Forgive me, my dear. Afraid I got my knickers in a twist again over those two. And it's the second time today!"

"I'm sorry I walked in but I heard the commotion and thought..."

11

"Oh, shoot, forget about walking in, honey. Door was probably open anyway, usually is. That lock's been broken forever. Been meaning to fix that."

She walked over to the door and closed it with some kind of special maneuver. "See, if you don't lift up on it when you close it, it doesn't shut right. And then all the heat gets out and I spend the next hour *kvetching* about it to the animals.

"They must get sick of it, but that's what I charge 'em in rent — listening to me whether they want to or not. They're stuck with the arrangement, poor babies. But it's not like they're gonna band together and go rent an apartment, is it?" She laughed at her own joke, then said, "Sorry I startled you."

With a small, yellow handkerchief she pulled from somewhere out of her sleeve, she mopped her forehead and laughed again.

"Surprised you though, didn't I? I'm still pretty smooth for an old broad with creaky bones. At least that's what I tell myself. And since there's nobody around to argue with me, I pretend that makes me right."

She held out her hand. "Name's Persephone, but you can call me Peri. Everybody else does.

"Hope it's not too warm in here for you. Can't stand the cold," she said, shoulders scrunching up. "Had way too much of it when I was a kid in Minnesota, and now I've got a zero tolerance policy. Like to crank up the fireplace and tiki torches out on the patio. Keep them blazing almost half the year."

I nodded and said, "That's an interesting name you have. *Persephone.* Don't think I've ever known anybody by that name before."

"No, probably not. It's unusual, that's for sure. My mother was a poet, writer and philosopher, in love with words and classical literature.

"She was especially in love with Greek mythology and that's where the name Persephone came from. But not one kid in a hundred at my school could pronounce it, much less spell it, so I just nicknamed myself Peri and that solved that."

"I'm not too up on my mythology, I'm afraid."

"Oh, don't worry about it. Nobody is these days. If it ever needs telling, I'll be happy to do so but it's not important right now.

"Anyway, it's nice to meet you, Helen," Peri said, putting down her broom to shake my hand. I couldn't help but notice how the thick gold band on her right middle finger glinted, even in the fading afternoon light of winter.

"How about having some tea with me and we can chat. It's kind of chilly today. A good day for a nice cup of tea."

"Yes. Thanks, that would be nice." I said, following Peri down the hallway to the kitchen. "Again, I'm sorry about barging in unannounced like that."

"Don't give it another thought, my dear. I've been expecting you. I meant to greet you at the door, but I got busy with my orchids, and then the damned bird and the damned cat. Well, you know how it is when you're doing something you love.

"The orchids, I mean, not chasing the animals. You lose track of time, but enough about that. Let's have a cup of tea, and then we'll take a look at my poor old garden out back."

Peri had one of those smiles that transform a face. It pillowed her cheeks from ear to ear, lifting her clear, blue eyes into a pair of lopsided ovals of well-traced lines.

As she talked she smoothed her marmalade hair with the absentminded touch of someone who had performed the ritual thousands of times.

"Did you come a long way?" she asked, adjusting her big sweater, a bulky pullover the color of smoke and irises.

"Well, not so far. I rode my bike. Why? Do I look a mess?"

Peri laughed. It was a lively, gentle laugh...kind and happy. "No, kiddo, you look fine. I was just wondering if you live nearby, that's all."

"Sorry. I get a little nervous with new people. I tend to blurt things out sometimes without thinking."

"I used to have a little of that in me, too, when I was your age. One of the best things about getting old is that it gets you over the minutia. Like being a bright redhead when you're seventy-nine. But you know what, who cares?

"It's not like I've got the Marine Marching Band lined up in the street to take me out dancing. Last week I was a sassy platinum, but I got bored with that pretty quick."

Peri was obviously having a great time being alive, something I secretly wished I knew how to do.

"A bit of something sweet with your tea, dear?" Peri asked, offering me a plate of desserts.

I chose a small slice of banana bread, thanked Peri and looked out the window, waiting for my tea to cool.

A few moments later, Peri said, "Drink up, dear. It'll take away the chill and then we will have had tea together, and we won't be new people to each other anymore."

I nodded, had a sip, and then answered the question from before. "You asked about where I live? It's about three miles from here on the cul-de-sac over on the other side of the hill. I just moved there a few months ago."

"Cul-de-sac, oh, that would be Oak Street," Peri said, nodding. "Well then, it wouldn't be too much of a hike for you to come to work."

"No, not much," I told her, a little hesitantly. "Not once I get used to it."

"Every time I look out this window at those sweet butterfly blossoms," Peri said with a big sigh, "I remember why I love this part of the country so much.

"A bougainvillea just about never goes barren here. That big girl out there gets sun all year long and just keeps flowering and flowering unless it's an unusually cold winter."

For the next half-hour, Peri and I sat and drank tea and talked about gardening. She explained that she owned this property and the house we were sitting in. Her land also included a large, walled garden that she'd cultivated from bare ground many years before.

The more Peri talked, the more I wanted the job. That is, until the worrying started. I worried that something would go wrong. I worried that I might not be able to keep up my end. I worried that I would get bored. I worried that if I took the job I might regret it.

But even in the state of mind I was in back then, I knew that these worries were nothing more than little lies I told myself because I was afraid. Afraid of what, I'm not even sure, disappointment maybe? Or hurt? Or failure? Or getting close to someone?

In the end though, all those lame ideas about what scared me didn't matter because the truth is, I needed to *do something* more than I needed to be afraid.

And besides, this quirky old woman with her orchids and tiki torches and bird and cat wars made me feel good in a way I hadn't felt for a long time. With a bit of luck, I thought, maybe she would hire me after all.

I listened as Peri began explaining the situation. "I live alone, quite contentedly now, raising flowers in and around the house and of course fooling around with my precious animals.

"But I stopped tending the garden years ago when, well that's a story I'll tell you later. Anyway, I've got some arthritis in my hands now, so even though I'm ready to go in and bring the garden back to life, I need another pair of hands."

As I listened, my eyes swept the pleasantly cluttered room, resting on a white orchid, a *phalenopsis*, Peri would tell me later, set out in a ceramic container in front of the bougainvillea-framed picture window. It bloomed in the midday sun that also bathed me in its light. It was a moment I could almost have eaten.

"If you're finished with your tea, Helen, why don't you and I take a look at my garden? But I have to forewarn you that it's quite a mess."

We put on our jackets and walked out the back door of the kitchen and around the outside of the house to a thick wooden gate behind some large bushes and pine trees.

A big brass lock fastened the hasp. Peri took a key from her pocket, unlocked the gate, and pushed the door inward. It creaked on its rusty hinges, then opened before us into a tangle that was more thorn than green. Still, it was a glorious, living ruin of a garden and this once-great creation held a quiet so full and calm, I instantly made it my own.

I *knew* I belonged in that garden. I can't tell you how I knew, but I knew. The pull of it on my heart was so real, so powerful.

Just as the door swung open, I could have sworn I heard my name, the sound floating to me as softly as a feather on the wind.

An instant later, a streak of color caught my eye as a cardinal flashed past, diving from the highest oak tree, crying softly as he skimmed the perimeter of the garden. In that moment, something awoke inside me, and all I wanted was to be in the garden and stay forever.

I turned to Peri, "Even if your garden *is* a bit disheveled, I love it here."

"Me, too. You can find your *Whole Self* in the silence and quiet growth of a place like this."

When Peri said the words *"Whole Self,"* I felt a strange natural power expanding in my chest like the endless blue of a summer sky. Something big was beginning, and I sensed it.

"Come on, let's go further in," Peri said, touching me lightly on the shoulder. "My great grandnieces are coming to stay with me this summer. Before they get here, I want to see the garden back in order."

She smiled her sweet smile and rolled up the sleeves of her sweater. "As I told you, these old fingers don't work so well anymore, but with your help, we can put it back together. I'm very sure that I'm not quite done with gardening yet."

We walked the length of the old garden that was bordered by three walls made of stone, one in the front and two on the sides.

There was no back wall as the garden gradually sloped down to a small river running by at the bottom. Just at the point where it began to turn from view, it curved into an inlet where a little blue sailboat was docked, rocking gently back and forth, up and down with the current.

Peri pointed to the water. "That river down there is the Little Dreamy. Pretty thing, isn't it? Full of fish and turtles, and there are hundreds of ducks on it every summer.

"A river's the simplest thing in the world, yet the most complex thing in the world at the same time. It's all of creation flowing by. Life just going where it's going."

Peri gestured in a sweeping motion toward the overgrowth. "But as for this mess, as you can see, there's a lot of work to be done. Think you want to take it on?"

I looked around the garden and down at the Little Dreamy. Without turning back to face her, I nodded and said without hesitation, "Yes, I do."

Peri nodded back and grinned. For some reason, I'm not quite sure why, Peri's term, *Whole Self,* hit me again, and I knew instinctively that I was in for more than just a gardening job.

When that thought had made it about half the way across my mind, Peri laughed softly, as if she had heard every word. I turned around to face her.

Then it happened again. Another rabbit hole moment!

For just a split second, as with Virgie in those last few moments outside the bus, a flash of red silk, as if Peri were clothed in a hooded cape or gown, with a bright burst of sunlight bouncing off her golden ring. But when I finished turning, there was Peri, looking just as she always had. I had to shake my head to rattle my brain back into gear.

"Everything okay, Helen?"

"Um, yes. It's nothing. I think I'm just a little tired from the long day I had yesterday and the ride up the hill today. But I'm all right."

Peri smiled and nodded. "Okay, then we'll start tomorrow. Glad you're here, Helen."

"Me too, Peri. I know you don't know me from Adam, so thanks for taking a chance on me."

"Oh, I think I have a pretty good line on who you are, Helen, and I like what I see. Wouldn't hire you if I weren't certain that this is a fit for both of us. You run along home now dear and we'll get started early tomorrow. Eight o'clock sound all right?"

"You bet. I'll be here, Peri. See you then."

SEVEN DOORS OF THE FIREMAKER

CHAPTER 3

THE GARDEN

I came back to Peri's the next day, and the day after that, and many more days after *that*, working here and there in the garden, often deep into the most forlorn and tangled parts.

It was hard at first, almost too hard because I wasn't in the best shape, but that had more to do with me than with the job. In those days, just about everything wore me out.

But it got easier after a while, and in some strange way I didn't fully yet understand, it was incredibly comforting being there. It was if I was one of those disheveled, neglected plants becoming healthier and stronger as the gardening progressed.

Peri gave me lots of room, which also accounts, in part, for how comfortable I felt. She didn't bark orders at me or ask a bunch of intrusive questions.

Mostly, I was left to choose the tasks I wanted to accomplish each day. I would spend time with her in the greenhouse tending her "orchid children," or the job I liked most of all, pressing further and further into the garden's most tangled overgrowth.

That time by myself, knowing Peri was nearby if I needed her, was like a balm to the hurt roiling around just under my skin.

And when we *did* work directly together or rest together in the late afternoon in front of her fireplace, Peri's presence, at times as wild as the garden, at times as steady as the Little Dreamy, blanketed me in safety and a feeling that was as close to joy as I had come in a long time.

I didn't know then how it was that Peri understood what I needed, but she did. She knew it was going to take me time to get the hang of things, just as she also knew I was there for more than a job and that I was in serious need of healing.

When I was tired or a little blue, she would encourage me to grab one of her cats and go sit under a certain especially large Live Oak tree she'd named Aunt Betty.

With my head resting against Aunt Betty's massive trunk and a cat purring in my lap, I could almost feel the current of life, flowing like the Little Dreamy, back and forth between the river, the tree, the cat, and me.

As I cleared and planted, my mind drifted with the flow of the days into memories of my difficult and lonely childhood.

I was the youngest of four children and the only girl in a family every bit as confused and thorny as Peri's garden. But in spite of that, I could also remember a time when I felt differently about life, a time when I felt light from within.

Back then, life seemed bursting with possibilities and I woke up every morning ready to greet them. But somehow, somewhere along the way, that Inner Light had dimmed and clouded over. All that was left was a kind of hazy malaise that seemed to drain the joy out of everything.

I wasn't ready to tell you about my childhood in much detail before. But by now, you have a pretty good idea of the state I was in when I came to Peri's house, so it might be helpful to know how I got that way. It's not all than uncommon a situation, sadly.

The events on the unhappy planet of my child-hood chipped away at something vital in the center of my being. Instead of being filled with color and song and joy, I was filled with sadness and illness and giving up.

Every hurt, every neglect left wounds in places no one else could see. Years of hiding in plain sight, years of not being seen by my family for who I really was, taught me how to be resigned to a small, truncated existence.

Oh sure, for a long time I did my best to resist, to fight for my truth and the right to *be*. But in the end the battle overwhelmed me and darkness seeped in through the cracks in my being.

Still, I can remember a time before that happened, a time when I was all questions and shining eyes.

I must have been about five when I asked my mother the most important question of my little life thus far. And I'll admit she gets credit for a good try on this, too. Better than on most of her tries, even if her astrophysics *were* a little flawed.

Obviously it's impossible to remember it exactly, but our conversation went something like this:

"Mom, how did the world get here?"

"The world? You mean how did the planet come to be?"

"Yes, how did the world get born?"

My mother hesitated, then said, "Well, a long, long time ago, when the sun was a lot bigger than it is now, a big explosion happened. Nobody really knows why.

"But it shook everything in the sky and knocked a chunk of the sun off and that broke into a thousand pieces. Those pieces went spinning into space, and one big fat piece started spinning around and cooling down until it became the world."

"And what about the rest of the pieces? Where did they go?"

"They went all over the place and made some other planets, I guess."

"Did any pieces fall down on the ground *after* our piece started being the world?"

By this time the big needle on my mother's Brief-Interpersonal-Moments-With-My-Beloved-Daughter meter was in the red zone.

"Lord, Helen, I don't know! This is just exactly the reason I never do this with you. One question answered leads to fifty million more. If you're so damned curious, why don't you go outside and see if you can find a little piece of the sun.

"It's time for me to watch *Days of Our Lives*, anyway. Bring me a glass of iced tea and then get out of here and go play."

I was used to that last part, and besides, I pretty much had what I wanted from her anyway. So, I got her iced tea and out I went to spend the rest of the day wandering around in a little haze trying to sort through the information I'd gleaned.

Because my mother had said so, it must at least be *possible* that there was a tiny piece of the sun lying around *somewhere*. And if it was out there just lying around somewhere, and somewhere could be *anywhere*, it was also possible I could find it.

And dipping further into my innocent childhood logic, if a person found something as magical as a small piece of the sun, then it followed that something absolutely wonderful was bound to happen, right?

I spent the whole afternoon searching our tree-lined street, which was the entire universe to me, thinking I would find *something*, some evidence that what my mother said was true. There might be a dark burn mark on a lawn or a little crater behind the grocery store, right? Something.

Nothing happened that day, or the next, or the next. But I still spent that whole summer in hot pursuit of a little shard of the sun. Of course, I didn't find it, but with a pack of mean older brothers and the kind of parents I had, what my search *did* provide was endless fodder for family ridicule.

Helen's hunt for a piece of the sun became the cruel and humiliating game my family never tired of at dinner. Before it was over, I'd stuffed that longing deep inside and begun to pretend it didn't matter.

That was where the trouble began, *pretending* it didn't matter. Over the course of my life, I became an expert at stuffing my longings and pretending they didn't matter.

Looking back now, with adult eyes, I realize that despite the pain of that experience and my eventual capacity to camouflage my feelings, something vital and worthwhile survived the process.

My longing for a greater understanding about what life meant and how it all worked stayed with me. And, I continued in my own way to search for what I suspected was out there, even though I couldn't see it.

When school started that year, I secretly kept looking for my piece of the sun. I looked in places both obvious and obscure. I looked in books and maps, and in poems and dreams. I sought my answer in things that called to me from a deep quiet distance.

Maybe, I thought, *maybe* I would find the meaning of things by looking where it wasn't so bright, where the shadows and the moon and the night sky stars would welcome my silent search. As with so many people, the years passed and the ultimate understanding I so desperately sought didn't come.

After a while, I almost forgot about that primal day and a time when I truly believed in something. Yet even forgetting what had started my search didn't completely banish the vague-but-persistent suspicion that I would find the answer somewhere, someday.

I learned to look closely at the little things because the seemingly insignificant things sometimes revealed an underlying truth or universal law that led to bigger and better places to search.

It seemed to me that if I just stayed awake, noticed the great and the small, and kept on expecting to find something important in all of it, there was at least a chance that one day I'd find what I had lost of myself. Then I would be whole again just as I had been when I was living the little girl version of me.

That seemed like a reasonable idea, but finding that place wasn't so easily done. By the time I was ten, instead of waking up ready to greet the day, the questions would start before I even had time to yawn.

"Why am I the way I am? What do I need? Why do I feel all broken and scattered? What am I doing here, anyway?"

But the answers just wouldn't come.

Over time, something akin to the exact opposite of my little piece of the sun, a shard of a small cold planet all my own, formed in the center of my chest. Over the years it grew into a hurt that never left, that organ called *pain* that I was talking about before.

Eventually, it was as if it had always been there, and worse, it had no intention of leaving. It would take a very specific lesson later on from the most unusual of sources to show me exactly what I must to do be rid of it.

Years later, as a teenager, a pivotal night came that would lead to that source.

I'm not quite sure anymore what happened that day. It was some argument or upset around the house — I don't exactly remember. I just know I was exhausted emotionally and physically. When I went to bed I knew I was heading into a deep, deep sleep.

But when I arrived at that nether place between sleep and waking, a quiet, gentle voice spoke to me.

It seemed to come from somewhere inside my room but at the same time from inside my head. The voice said:

*"I am The Firemaker.
Seek me and you will find me.
Find me and you will be whole."*

Needless to say, it scared the heck out of me! I mean it's not as if a disembodied voice talks to you every day, is it? I sat up so quickly I banged my head on the bedpost and nearly fell on the floor.

Later, when I'd calmed down a bit and realized just what had happened, my fears turned to downright elation. At least *something* was responding to my pain, even though I had no idea what it was.

Of course, my next realization was that I had absolutely no idea what the mysterious statement meant, much less where I was supposed to start looking for this "Firemaker," whoever, or whatever, it was.

I lay awake for several hours hoping the voice would speak again and offer more clues, but there was nothing more. After thinking it over for a while, though, I realized that in a way, it didn't matter that the voice didn't return. I knew that I would leave home the next day, regardless. It was time, and knowing that was what mattered.

And I knew that I'd find The Firemaker if it took the rest of my life, whatever it required. Having made those decisions, to leave home and search for The Firemaker, relaxed me to the core and I quickly fell asleep.

As I slept I dreamt of a place so incredibly warm and alive, a place so much a part of me that wherever I went in the dream, it transformed into what I knew was my true home. I never saw her in the dream, but I knew instinctively that The Firemaker was there with me, close by but unseen.

And that somehow, some way, I would find her and learn what I really needed to know to be whole and have a full and wonderful life.

SEVEN DOORS OF THE FIREMAKER

CHAPTER 4

THE LITTLE DREAMY

At the end of each workday in the garden, long after the light had gone, Peri and I would sit together by the fire, taking in the evening and the cool, moist air that blew in off the Little Dreamy.

Although Peri disliked the cold, she always kept a window open just a bit so the breeze could come in and the cats could call her through the screen to come open the back door.

Bundled up in a blanket on the green sofa, I reveled in the river's soft sound and the fresh air in my lungs. In Nature's whispered kiss, I heard evening's promise that I would soften too.

Spring was approaching. She would come first with paper whites and hyacinths. The crocuses had already pierced the hard winter ground. Soon their tiny, hopeful heads would send brilliant explosions of saffron and yellow bursting into the garden. The green-budded fruit trees and first strawberries would not be far behind. And, then, the violets would come.

Out there, just beyond the limits of my vision, the Little Dreamy ran downstream to the ocean. Just knowing that, just embracing that inevitable reunion of fresh water with its mother, the Sea, delivered a calm I'd longed for but never known.

The sound of the river told me I was in the right place in my search for The Firemaker. The Little Dreamy was making its way home...and so could I.

CHAPTER 5

ALTARS

A s I said earlier, just like Alice in her trip through Wonderland, I was well into my journey before I fully knew it.

In some ways, it started the day my mother told me about the piece of the sun and continued when the voice spoke to me, when I left home, when I met Virgie, and when I went to work for Peri.

But the day my search for The Firemaker *really* moved into high gear was the day I was standing in Peri's garden steadily cutting back the tangled mass of bushes growing along the southern wall.

Suddenly the clippers clanked in a way that was different from the noise they normally made when they hit the stone walls.

Parting the leaves, I slowly opened an area to the light and found, much to my surprise, a small stone alcove. Much wider at the bottom than at the top, the recess sloped upward to a gently curving point, creating a tiny altar in the garden wall.

I continued to cut away the tangled growth until I uncovered a small square ceramic tile about four inches by four inches at the base of the alcove.

When I brushed the dirt away I could see a child's drawing of some kind of wheel had been painted on the tile, then glazed and fired.

"Peri?"

"Uh-huh?"

"Can you come here a second? I found something interesting."

Peri took off her gloves, leaned her spade against a wall and walked over to me. She gently stroked the small tile as though it were a living thing and smiled broadly.

"You found one of the little altars! Told you this garden was full of secrets."

"You mean there are others?"

"Oh, yes. I had them built in when the walls were being done. There are seven of them, all covered up like this one I'm afraid."

"Where'd the tiles come from, Peri?"

"Well, my sister's girls did them when they were little. We used to have a small kiln back here. Made ceramics, little pinch pots and these tiles and such. I'd like to do something along those lines when *their* girls come this summer."

"I like it. It's very sweet."

"Thanks, honey. Yes, they are sweet. It sure will be nice to have them out in the light again." Peri patted my arm and went back over to her spade.

There was something completely delightful about having discovered the little altar. It let me know that the garden was starting to take shape, to reveal its treasures, and so was I.

I felt good about what I'd accomplished, but even better about how Peri was becoming a friend and mentor. As I said, unlike most of my previous employers, she gave me plenty of room. She didn't hover or want more than we'd agreed upon.

That method worked wonders with me and I found myself, maybe for the first time in my life, settling in. There was a pride I took in it all, a warm, clean feeling that in large part because of my work, Peri and her family would fully enjoy the garden again.

Over the next few weeks, I uncovered five more altars in the side garden walls, each with a different tile, just as Peri had said.

Peri had chosen to leave the overgrowth inside the front entrance wall for last, and it was there that I found the seventh altar. But when I found that final one, the tile was missing.

I called out to Peri to let her know I'd uncovered the last altar and to ask if she knew where it was. "This altar doesn't have a tile, Peri. Do you remember what happened to it?"

A shadow seemed to fall on Peri's face as she let out a deep sigh. "There's a reason why I put off clearing up the front entrance wall for last and why this altar was never finished. Come with me to the potting shed. I think I still have...well, just come along and I'll explain."

We walked out of the garden and back toward the house. Just outside the back porch was a small potting shed where all the materials and tools for gardening were stored.

I'd been in there many times but had never had any reason to open the small cabinet on the back wall. Peri opened it and inside were two ceramic tiles, one with a drawing of some kind of flower and the other with an image of a candle. She reached in, took them out, and handed them to me.

"Here you go, honey. Take these home with you tonight and you decide which one to put up in the last altar. I really don't have a preference.

"You see, what I haven't told you is that my husband, Edward, passed away in the garden before we had time to cement in the last tile."

"Oh, Peri! I'm so sorry. I had no idea."

"No, of course not, dear. I never told you because it's still painful. Some things you just never quite get over no matter what. We were so happy being together, happy as clams on the beach, so losing him was pretty hard to take.

"As you can imagine, the garden took a long, long time to create. We loved working on it and playing with our nieces out there down by the Little Dreamy so we were in no hurry. We worked on it for years.

"Ed and I were out working one sunny fall day, just the two of us. The girls had made two tiles before they went home at summer's end and left them in the kiln to be fired.

"Actually, that was creating a bit of a dilemma for us. There was only one altar left to decorate, but both girls had made a tile so, well, we weren't sure exactly *what* we were going to do. As it turned out, that decision never had to be made.

"Anyway, we were doing all the stuff you and I do, planting, watering, pruning, all of that. I was down at the back on the open end of the garden, and

36

Ed was sitting against the front wall beneath that last altar.

"I called to him to bring down some potting soil but he didn't answer. It was such a lazy day, I thought he'd just gone to sleep, so I didn't pay much attention at first. But then I got the strangest feeling.

"I walked up and called his name and nudged his shoulder but he didn't stir. I knew right then that he was dead, but I shook him and tried to revive him anyway. Nothing worked. The doctors said his heart just stopped, that it happens sometimes.

"No warning, and thank God, no pain. He just sat down for a little snooze and never woke up again. Never had a single symptom. So you see, it was a lot more than arthritis that stopped my gardening.

"After Ed's funeral, I locked the garden gate and went on an extended trip. When I got back home I just couldn't come out here again, not until the day before you arrived.

"But this experience was something I wanted to give to my grandnieces like we'd done for their mothers. So sprucing up the garden and reliving the memories of Ed and the girls, and letting the garden nurture someone like you, well, I didn't want to leave any of that untouched before I die.

"And it turned out that you were the perfect person to accompany me through this rebirth of the garden. I knew it the moment I laid eyes on you. Old Virgie has pretty good instincts. She was right to send you to me."

"I'm so sorry for your loss, Peri. Now it all makes sense. There's more to that Virgie than meets the eye, isn't there?"

"Oh, yes! Lots more. She's a real treasure, and one of my dearest friends.

"I'm a very strong woman, Helen, if I do say so myself, but losing Ed nearly killed me. Just when I needed a friend most, I literally bumped into Virgie at a swap meet and we just hit it off. She's a widow, too, you know. Her husband was killed in Vietnam when they were just a couple of teenagers.

"After the swap meet, we had coffee and she told me how she came to understand that being widowed was just life putting her on a different path, an inner journey and one I could go on as well, if I wanted to take it. And take it I did. Now, thanks to Virgie, that journey inside is something I absolutely cherish. It's made me whole despite losing Ed.

"Still, some things just have their own life cycle, their own time frame, and nothing you do can speed it up. I miss Ed terribly because we were such wonderful friends. But I've made my peace with his passing and I imagine him off doing something lovely on the other side. I'll catch up with him soon enough.

"For years, though, my work was inside *me*, not in the garden, and I knew that I would know when it was time to open it up and go back to work. And I was right. Lots of people answered the ad that you answered. But when you called, I knew you were the one and came out and entered the garden again that same day for the first time in forever.

"Sure enough, it's a true pleasure to be working in the garden again, and especially to share it with you."

"Oh, Peri, thank you so much for telling me. The garden means even more to me now, and I was already in love with it, and you. You are the dearest, sweetest friend. Thank you for sharing all this with me."

"My pleasure, Helen. I feel the same about you. Now enough about the past and my troubles. You put these tiles in your backpack and scoot on home. Sun's starting down and I don't want you out on that bike tonight. Looks like it might be clouding up to rain."

SEVEN DOORS OF THE FIREMAKER

CHAPTER 6

GRAVITY AND THE YELLOW BICYCLE

Peri was right, it had rained during the night, so the roads were still wet that next morning when I rode my bicycle toward her house.

I was coming down the last part of the steep hill, gliding into the abrupt turn at the bottom when, out of nowhere, a little girl dashed into the street after a soccer ball.

Slamming on the brakes, I somehow managed to miss her but turned too sharply to keep my balance. All I remember is that the bike shot out from under me, and I went flying. I landed hard on my back, rolled over, skidded on my side, and finally crashed, headfirst, into the concrete curb.

As I lay on the ground, my thoughts went to Peri, the garden, the little altars with their lovely tiles.

Then everything faded away into nothing.

SEVEN DOORS OF THE FIREMAKER

CHAPTER 7

BABY STEPS

My first awareness after the accident was of a warm wind and the whispering of leaves. At first I thought I imagined it, but then, there it was—the same voice I'd heard in my bedroom all those years ago.

"Wake up, Helen."

I sat up and felt my head for bumps, scrapes or blood, but everything seemed fine and stranger still, there was no pain whatsoever. I looked around, blinking in bewilderment.

I was in Peri's garden, that much I knew, yet it was so different. The garden had shed all signs of winter and the air, now warm and bright, was scented with sweet perfume. It couldn't be, but it was. It was summer.

"Where am I?"

"You are in The Garden."

"Yes, I see that, but it's...it's changed. How could the seasons change like this?" I paused, trying to collect my senses. "And how did I get here?"

"Never mind that just now. The Garden is what you need it to be at this moment, and I am here to help."

The voice seemed to come from all around as before, but from inside my head as well—very strange. In my confusion, I turned, searching for the source of the voice. "Who are you?" I called out. "Where are you?"

"I am The Firemaker. You have been seeking me for a long time, have you not?"

"Oh my gosh! You're The Firemaker?" I said. *Could it be? Finally?*

"I can't believe it! I've been looking for you forever in one way or another. But where are you? I can hear you but I can't see you."

"Turn toward the live oak tree you call Aunt Betty."

I turned toward that favorite old tree and saw a tall, lean woman standing under the overhang in the very center of the garden. A red silk gown with a hood covered her shoulders and arms, its hem reaching the ground.

The shadows of the tree and the hood obscured the woman's face, but when she moved her right hand, a bright flash of sunlight reflected off the gold ring on her middle finger.

I stared for a moment, drinking in the sight of her, before stammering out, "I—I—how long have you been standing there?"

"I've always been here."

"You've *always* been here? I've never seen you."

44

"Your eyes were closed to me. Your ears heard my call but once. Even so, I've been here, speaking to you all the same."

"Then why can I see and hear you now?"

"Perhaps you already know why."

A chill ran up my spine. "Oh, no! Don't tell me. I fooled around and did it. I'm dead, aren't I? I finally pushed the limits on that danged bike once too often and now I've killed myself. I'm such an idiot!"

The Firemaker laughed softly. "No, Helen, you're not dead. Nor are you, in your words, an idiot. You are simply *ready*."

"I'm not dead?"

"No, you're very much alive."

I could feel the muscles in my neck and back start to relax. "Whew! Thank God. Well then, if I'm not dead what *is* this? I *must* be dreaming because something way beyond weird is happening to me."

The Firemaker laughed again. "Believe me, you're not dreaming, Helen. This is your *natural* state of being, even though it's not the state of consciousness you would call normal.

"In truth, what you call normal is a dream. But that's a long story and not the important thing now.

"In any case, all you need to know is that you're standing here, just a few steps from the Land Behind the Doors, in a state of readiness."

"The Land Behind the Doors? A state of readiness?" I was starting to panic just a little.

"Readiness for what?"

In the years I'd spent imagining this moment, I had never thought past *finding* The Firemaker. It had never once occurred to me that I'd have to *do something* once I found her, especially something

45

that involved going to a place called the Land Behind the Doors.

"If you decide to take the journey that awaits, in due course you'll understand that, and much, much more. But these things can't be explained simply. You will have to work to understand."

I nodded my head as if that was going to alleviate my misgivings, started to ask for a reprieve because I sensed that this was no lightweight event, then finally just shut up and accepted the challenge. I knew I couldn't walk away, but I still needed some time to think.

"Okay, but can we please slow down a little? The last thing I remember was riding my bike, and a little girl ran into the street after her ball, and I tried to avoid her but I crashed, I think, and, well, suddenly here I am and it's summer.

"It's a lot to take in. I'll need a few minutes to get my bearings, if that's all right."

"Of course. Take all the time you need."

That calmed me down and I suddenly remembered there was something very important I had to know.

"If it's okay, there's something I have to ask. What does it mean, your name or title or whatever it is, *The Firemaker*?"

"If you do the work you'll know all about that in due time. That's all I that can tell you at this point because you would never understand it now. Much preparation is required, you see."

"Preparation? Preparation for what?"

"For living your life differently. Isn't it true you've been unhappy with things as they are? Isn't it true that you've long sought a new way of being?"

I nodded. "Yes, it's true. I've been looking for a new way. Even before you spoke to me in my room that night when I was a teenager, I was looking. I didn't really know what I was after, but I was most certainly looking. It's not like I've ever been what you would exactly call *content*."

"Yes, Helen, I know. But this learning, this journey, if you complete it, will change your life forever. You'll never have to go back to the way things were. It won't even be possible to go back."

"How can you be so sure? All I seem to do is climb halfway up a mountain and then abruptly slide right back down. Now that I'm here, even though I think I want to, I'm not so sure I can do what you ask. What *are* you asking of me, anyway?"

"See the doors along The Garden wall?"

I looked at what had once been small stone altars with children's tiles embedded in them. Now they had become full-sized doors.

"What happened to the little altars?"

"Changed. This is the place for change. Those are very, very special doors, Helen."

"In what way?"

"In order to complete your transformation, you must pass through seven doors and experience whatever awaits on the other side of each. Some of it will be thrilling, some of it unsettling, but all of it will be worthwhile. And if you make it through seven doors, you'll undergo a metamorphosis as radical as that from chrysalis to butterfly."

I thought for a moment. "Please, Firemaker, I hope you don't take this the wrong way but, is *quitting* allowed?"

"Yes, Helen. In these tasks, you will be allowed to exercise your free will for with this journey or not. You can end it at any point. But, if you choose to go forward, know that I will never be far away, even if you cannot see me. It will be as it has always been even though you didn't know it." The Firemaker's voice was warm and encouraging.

"Now you must decide."

"Okay. Just give me a few minutes, all right?"

The Firemaker nodded.

I walked over and sat down under Aunt Betty with my back leaning against her massive, ancient trunk for support. I thought about what I'd experienced in my life, about how disillusioned I'd been so much of the time. It was obvious to me that, other than Peri and my gardening job, there was nothing much for me to go back to.

Don't get me wrong, Peri and the lovely garden were wonderful. More than wonderful, but obviously they weren't all I needed to build my whole life around.

Something enormously important was missing, even if I didn't know what it was. I got up, turned and faced The Firemaker. Well, *faced* might not be the proper word because, as I was to learn, I would not see her face for a very long time.

"You've made your decision?"

It was unlike me to make decisions quickly back then, but for some reason I didn't hesitate.

"Yes," I told her, "I have. I want to try this. I want *so much* for my life to change. But you should know I have serious doubts about whether I can pull it off.

"I have no idea what's ahead and yet I've already got the feeling I'm probably not the best person for such a grand journey, especially to some mysterious place called the Land Behind the Doors."

"Be easy with yourself, Helen. It took great effort to even reach this starting place. Be pleased that you found your way here at all and please don't be too concerned with whether you'll finish or do well. Whatever you get done will be transformational and very beneficial, I assure you.

"There's time to rest before we begin. There's even time for you to change your mind. Just be still within yourself and leave your worries at the foot of this old tree. She'll comfort and calm you.

"See the green hammock? Spend some time there. When you're ready, walk The Garden's path and try to really look, really see. Let The Garden show you Life. You'll know if this is meant to be, and exactly when it's time to begin your journey."

So, I stayed.

And while time wasn't really time in The Garden, I remained there for what seemed like weeks, dozing in the green hammock, daydreaming under a coverlet of dandelions and daisies. I meandered down the path, following the trails of beetles and flights of dragonflies. The Firemaker was always nearby but said little.

I thought my time in Peri's garden had rested me from the chronic weariness that hovered over me like a bad climate, but here in The Garden with The Firemaker, I could see there was more to my fatigue than I knew. It ran deep. Soul deep.

Even if nothing more had happened beyond spending that special time in The Garden, I believe just being there would have transformed me because everywhere, absolutely *everywhere*, was LIFE. And for the first time, I was truly seeing it.

Many trees grew in The Garden, not just Live Oak, but also Liquid Amber and Willow and Fruit Sisters, Orange and Grapefruit, their sturdy branches bent low with sweetness, aching to be picked.

Nearby, Poppy pushed up, fire red, through The Garden's rich soil. Skimming the green, Quick Sparrow said hello to Buttercup and Rose. Hummingbird joined them, kissing the nectar from Jasmine and Lily. Green serpent vines, heavy with ripe cantaloupe beads wound through Morning Glory, crossing fields of Marigold, Starling and Junegrass.

Everything in The Garden answered summer's call, from the plants and the animals to the lush, cool, clover-covered slope of the hill and the pure, crystalline water of the Little Dreamy below.

Then, the moment of certainty came. Like a new-born foal that knows in an instant she can run, I knew that I was ready. I turned and glanced over my right shoulder. As usual, The Firemaker was there. I took a deep breath and whispered, "Now."

The Firemaker nodded and motioned toward the First Door.

CHAPTER 8

THE FIRST DOOR: THE WHEEL

The tile on the First Door was decorated with a painting of a wheel, not the kind on your car, but the lottery kind, the spin-and-take-your-chances kind.

I looked at the door and then at The Firemaker, although I knew I wouldn't see her face. I was used to that by now. In all the time I'd spent wandering the garden, I'd never seen more than a faint outline of her face in the shadows of the hood.

I glanced at the door again. "What do I do now?"

"Simply push it open and walk through. Not too fast and not too far. There's something on the other side you'll want to talk over with me."

"Okay, here goes." I pushed the door open and slowly stepped through, with The Firemaker following close behind. It didn't take long to see what I was up against. I was standing on a narrow ledge atop a steep cliff, several thousand feet high. I nearly fainted.

I quickly turned to run back through the door, but The Firemaker had already closed it behind us. Still, I pounded on the door, desperately hoping it would open somehow. I looked toward her, my heart racing, my mouth a wad of cotton, and pointed to the wide, empty sky.

"My God! This is a mistake! It has to be! Just *what* exactly do you expect me to do up here?"

"Well, first of all, why not try and get all you can out of the experience? Why not take a minute and enjoy the view?" She touched my arm and I immediately felt more centered, if not all that brave.

Summoning all my courage, I took a few slow, deep breaths to calm my racing pulse. I gently stepped closer to the edge near The Firemaker. The view was spectacular!

Sunrise opened the sky, staining it orange as it fanned out before us, over the distant valley below where a long line of people, looking no larger than ants, gathered at what looked to me like a country fair. It was lovely, but I was still so afraid of the height that my knees actually shook, not a very good way to start an adventure.

Suddenly, a terrible realization hit me. I knew what was next, or at least I thought so. "Wait a minute! Hold on! You don't really want me to climb down this cliff, do you?"

"No, not at all."

"Whew!" I laughed nervously. "*That's* a relief."

The Firemaker nodded. "Yes. I would imagine it is. What you have to do is jump."

"Jump? JUMP??? I don't think so! I'm very willing to follow you *within reason*, but I'm not jumping off this cliff, not for a gazillion dollars!"

"I understand, Helen," The Firemaker said quietly, almost tenderly. "But if not for the fear, you'd like to try wouldn't you?"

I peeked over the edge. "It's a little hard to imagine not having any fear."

"Yet you *have* managed to imagine this without fear. Don't you remember pretending to do this as a child? Leaping out, soaring like a hawk down into a pretty valley like this one? You've pretended that, haven't you?"

"Sure. But this situation is real and that was just make believe."

"There's less difference between the two than you might think, but I understand. Tell me, what do you think you would need to make it possible for you to take the leap?"

"Well, for one thing, a lot more good luck than I'm used to having."

The Firemaker opened the palm of her right hand and said, "Very well, take this pouch. It contains what you ask for. Here, let me hang it around your neck." She stepped around behind me and draped the strings of the pouch over my head. "There. All the luck you'll ever need. Now, are you ready to jump?"

"Wait, wait, WAIT!" I yelled, now nearly hysterical. "I don't care how much luck you've got stuffed inside that little pouch, it's not enough. I need something else, a rope or something. No, maybe a parachute."

As soon as I'd spoken the word "parachute," I felt the weight of a pack on my back and straps fastened to my body.

"How did you do that?"

The Firemaker said, "You might want to think of it as a method of advanced goal setting. If you manage to pass through seven doors, you will learn a Cosmic Law that explains it, but that's a long way off at this point. What is more important right now is your gear."

The Firemaker adjusted the parachute's harness a bit, then pointed to the cliff. "There you go, Helen. Now you can jump."

I held my hand up and stepped back as far from the edge as I could. "Hold on a minute. I haven't the slightest idea about parachuting. I have no clue how to do it."

"Yes, well, it's actually quite simple. You stand right there on that big rock and jump off."

"Then what?"

"Well, because of the Law of Gravity, you will immediately begin falling quite rapidly toward the ground."

"Hmmm. I assumed that. And then?"

"And then?"

"And then what do I do to keep from getting splattered at the bottom like a fat bug on a windshield?"

"After a while, you pull the cord. Here, let me place it in your hand. You yank it when you've had enough free fall. The longer you wait, the more exciting it is. That's all there is to it."

"But if it doesn't open, or I do it wrong, it'll kill me!"

The Firemaker laughed softly. "Just a short time ago you thought you were already dead. If I hadn't told you differently, you'd have thought *this* was the after life, correct?"

"Well, yes, I guess so."

"Then just pretend I was mistaken and that you're already dead. And besides," The Firemaker said, pointing to my neck, "you have your lucky pouch. I really don't see how you can lose."

"Yes, well, whatever's in there, I sure hope you put in some new batteries."

The Firemaker chuckled softly. "Try to relax, Helen. The pouch and parachute will work just fine. Simply follow the instructions I've given you and everything will come out perfectly, I assure you. Enjoy the ride."

SEVEN DOORS OF THE FIREMAKER

CHAPTER 9

SPINNING

I turned my attention to the edge for a split second and when I turned back with another question, The Firemaker was gone. My heart sank. I looked over my shoulder at the terrifying drop I was facing. It didn't look any better no matter what angle I took.

"Oh, mannnnnnnnnnnn! This is just dandy."

So there I was, completely terrified, alone, thousands of feet up with no escape, and no way off the ledge but to jump.

I decided that yanking on the door was a good idea, but when I did it was locked and now there was a sign that said, "OUT OF ORDER" with one of those little yellow smiley faces on it.

"Hilarious," I said to no one. Then I focused on my problem again.

"Crap! Crap! Crap!" I shouted, then spun around and timidly looked down the cliff face once more.

"FIREMAKER! Oh, FIREMAKER! I'd like to discuss this a little further!" I heard nothing but my own echo.

At my feet was a shelf of rock, jutting out barely far enough for me to stand on. Below was a sheer cliff with no trails and no way to climb down. After several more tries at the door and many looks down for some other way out, I finally surrendered to the situation.

Clutching the pouch in one hand and the ripcord in the other, I stepped out onto the boulder, took a deep breath, closed my eyes and leapt.

Trust me, I got over the thrill of free fall very quickly. I was barely off the cliff when I yanked the cord. The parachute opened with a loud *whop!* As it billowed and opened fully, I saw that I was going to be all right.

Just as The Firemaker had said it would be, I soon found the feeling wonderfully exhilarating, so much so that I laughed and kicked my feet as I drifted through the morning sky.

Several minutes later, I plopped down onto a huge waterbed sitting in the middle of a large open field. The parachute collapsed, covering me in nylon, or whatever they make those things out of these days, and I lay quietly, riding the waves of the waterbed until it was perfectly still.

"That was wonderful," I said to myself as I unbuckled the harness. The air had a slight chill to it, and I rubbed my shoulders to warm up, laughing as I rolled off the bed and onto my feet.

Far across the field people were lined up by the dozens at the gates of what I could now clearly see was an amusement park.

I began the long walk across the field. It was an easy stroll, flat and even with no rocks or gullies. Reaching the other side, I spoke to the first person I met, a sturdy soldier with a red beret. "What's going on? Why such a big crowd?"

"The Big Deal Wheel," she said.

"The what?"

"We've all come to try our hands at spinning the Big Deal Wheel. I'm telling you, everybody does it, absolutely everybody."

In the distance, I could see the giant Big Deal Wheel whirling round and round. It was a formidable sight, but the eager and hopeful faces of the people standing in line didn't seem the least bit apprehensive.

"Here," the soldier said, "jump in front of me. I'm sure nobody will mind."

I thanked her, but as I stepped in line the lady behind us had a fit.

"Hey! Just a minute, Sugarplum! What do you think *you're* doing? Wait your turn like everybody else! Who do you think you are?"

Sugarplum. That didn't sound like a very good start to our relationship.

The soldier turned around and snarled something nasty at the woman who growled back. They went at it for a full minute until I finally stepped out of line.

I said to the soldier, "Hey, look, it's not worth it. Thanks anyway."

I told the other lady I was sorry and headed for the end of the line. That didn't seem to help much because the two continued flinging insults at each other, but at least I wasn't in the middle of it.

When I finally reached the end of the line, I joined the others as they waited, moving ever closer to the Big Deal Wheel. It was perched in the exact center of a high stage with stairs on either end. People poured in, climbed the stairs, took a spin, and then walked off the opposite end of the stage.

Some of them, I noticed, smiled a big toothy grin of pleasure as they walked away. But others didn't seem nearly as happy. They left the stage with a dazed look and wild eyes, disappointment filling their hearts.

Above the Wheel a large, lime green banner was stretched across the length of the stage. It read:

THE BIG DEAL WHEEL
What goes around comes around.

And underneath that, just barely visible to the naked eye:

Caution! While this equipment is made of the finest materials, the manufacturer makes no warranty, implied or written concerning its use.

Spin at your own risk.

Dreams, Wishes & Surprises Industries, Inc.
Magic, Illinois.

As I waited, scores of people took their turns, and the line slowly inched forward. By now, it was afternoon and the air was stifling hot, but the crowd was still enthusiastic.

It became clear to me right away that the prizes being won were not always desirable, nor, for that matter, could they always even be counted on to go to the one who had just spun.

Some of the stuff was really quite ordinary, like small kitchen appliances, gardening tools and such. Some of it was really sweet, like an island vacation for two, or a cuddly little puppy, or a new summer dress. But some of it was not very nice, like flat tires, parking tickets, bad neighbors who steal your newspaper, life's annoying little nuisances.

But the truly unfortunate ones, well, I hate to tell you this, but they got stuck with things it would take the rest of their lives to forget or recover from.

"I didn't want that!" or "Yippee! I finally got it!" or "Why is this happening to me?" they yelled as old baseball gloves and faded hula-hoops landed on their heads. A storm of dried-up Christmas trees nearly suffocated a group right in front of the stage while a well-dressed woman in a business suit got a dented Viking helmet and a five-year term in prison for embezzlement.

Bad hair days, big splashy weddings, husbands who came home faithfully and wives who ran away. These and all kinds of other large and small triumphs and tragedies came into the lives of the spinners of the Big Deal Wheel.

I watched all of this for a long time before I had even the slightest clue what was really going on, before I began to sense that something connected these people to the things they received. It slowly became apparent that those who spun weren't the random winners or chance victims they first appeared to be.

It's hard explain how I knew...I just knew. But the more I watched, the more I realized that often the lucky ones felt entitled to great results while the unlucky ones believed they deserved bum goods.

It was all so plain, painfully so. Yet the possibility that *they played a major part* in calling the things they received to themselves had obviously never even occurred to most of them.

Interestingly, not every one, but *many* of those fortunate enough to get something truly wonderful returned immediately to the end of the line to try for something better. Despite showing tremendous enthusiasm at the moment they won, I realized that those people didn't *really value* what they got once they had it.

In fact, the more often they returned to the Wheel and spun, the less satisfied they became with what they already had, even if it were something you or I might die for.

For a few larger-than-life, ecstatic moments they had a shot at, well, *everything*. The anticipation of having something new, something light years better than what they already possessed was fabulous. No, it was better than fabulous, it was *intoxicating* and it was addictive.

And, as with all addictive things, the high didn't last long. That was the moment when they hopped right back in line for another turn.

After a while, though, I began to suspect that at least a few of the older folks knew they were out of control. The thrill they got from spinning the Wheel made them feel for a moment that they were living larger, more powerful lives, but it was obvious that spinning had become a completely joyless task.

I couldn't tell for sure, but I figured the reason they kept coming back was mostly because they were simply *used to it*. Maybe it never occurred to them there might be some place they could go for fulfillment other than the Wheel.

I was getting downright cocky about all this insight and wisdom I was crediting myself with when, all of a sudden, I found myself at the head of the line.

Mind you now, a lot of what I'm telling you I know only through hindsight. At the time the emotion I felt most was *conflicted*.

"Certainly," I reasoned, "The Firemaker guided me here for a purpose, even if I don't know what it is."

Yet the feeling that I should skip all this and press on kept growing inside me until I wasn't sure what to do. Something powerful told me there was an alternative to this that was better. Something said I should just walk away, right now, and forget it.

Instead, I stood there in one of my all-too-familiar clouds of indecision. As I got into full scale faltering mode, I suddenly had a sense of déjà vu. A vague memory of having been here before spiraled into my brain. Had *I* stood in front of the Big Deal Wheel before?

But insight and wisdom would have to wait because it was my turn to spin!

At last, I finally had a chance to get something good, something that might make me feel more alive inside! I told myself that a spin at the Big Deal Wheel might solve all my problems, might give me what I needed because, just like all the other people in the park, I needed something, wanted *something*. I just didn't know what.

The heat of the moment made it impossible to think clearly, and besides, the crowd was nudging me on, shouting, "Hurry Up! Hurry Up!" I lifted my arm to wipe the sweat from my forehead and wondered vaguely, "Why am I doing this?" But the crowd pressed forward, screaming in unison, "Spin the Wheel! Spin the Wheel! Spin the Wheel!"

"Everyone's waiting, what else can I do?" I said under my breath and began to climb the stairs. I must have been moving too slowly to suit the people behind me, though, because now the crowd was getting angry. I caught a glimpse of the soldier who had been so kind to me before. "Hurry up, dammit!" she shouted. "I gotta get a better boyfriend!"

Over the uproar and the pounding of my heart I couldn't hear any more of what the soldier was saying, but I probably wouldn't have liked it anyway. So, I grabbed a peg on the Wheel, tightened my body to gather the maximum force, and spun.

The Big Deal Wheel crackled and buzzed and whirred as it turned. A huge picnic basket full of baseballs flew out and knocked the soldier down. Then a brief thunderstorm of expired credit cards pelted several people in the crowd, and a tiny blue monkey leapt from shoulder to shoulder, yanking off men's toupees and peeing on women's shoes. It was nuts.

Finally, as the Wheel slowly stopped spinning, a small drawer popped open at the bottom. *Kaching!*

I reached in for my prize and pulled out the only thing there, a moldy fortune cookie.

I looked around, stunned. "This is it? A stupid fortune cookie? All this waiting and leaping off a cliff and all I get is a moldy fortune cookie?"

Now the crowd was wildly screaming. "Open it! Open it!" They yelled. So I broke the cookie open.

The crowd went silent and I heard the soldier shout, "What does it say?" as I read to myself:

GET THE HELL OFF THE STAGE!

I couldn't believe it, but there it was. I grimaced, shook my head, and held the little strip of paper up to show them. "Um, well…it says, 'Get the hell off the stage,' actually."

Immediately the crowd broke out in a chant like this was some kind of college football rally.

"Get the hell…off the stage! Get the hell…off the stage! Get the hell…off the stage!"

From the looks on their faces it was obvious that they weren't just repeating what I had read, either. They wanted me to get the hell off the stage. *Now.*

I made a nasty little face at them, stuck out my tongue, stuffed the strip of paper into my shirt pocket and hurled the crumbled fortune cookie at the crowd. "You people make me sick!" I yelled.

Stumbling across the stage, I went down the steps in a daze. Now what? I looked up at the faraway cliff where this adventure started, then around the valley. At last I spotted the waterbed and set out across the field toward it.

When I reached the waterbed several minutes later, I collapsed on top of it and drew the parachute up around me like a blanket. Just before giving myself over to sleep, I reached into my pocket, held the strip of paper to the sky and read it again just to make sure I wasn't mistaken. I wasn't.

I wadded up the paper, flicked it into the air and muttered to no one: "Big Deal."

CHAPTER 10

THE SECOND DOOR: THE PEARL

Exhausted after my ordeal at the Wheel, I settled into the waterbed and immediately fell into a deep sleep. When I awoke, I wasn't on the waterbed any more but back in The Garden in the green hammock hanging from the comforting branches of Aunt Betty. The Firemaker was standing nearby.

Normally I would have been puzzled out of my mind at how that could have happened, but by now, I was getting used to strange happenings around The Firemaker.

"Did you have an interesting time, Helen?"

"Very interesting, to say the least. And, safe to say, not quite what I expected."

"No, I suppose not. As I told you before, reality and fantasy aren't so different as one might imagine. Perhaps the First Door has helped you to begin to accept so-called *impossible* possibilities?"

"That's putting it mildly."

"After the First Door, how do you feel about this journey. Will you be staying for more?"

I thought for several seconds.

"To tell the truth, I really don't understand any of this, but even if I don't get it, the Big Deal Wheel was nothing if not interesting. So yes, Firemaker. I'll stay."

"Very good, Helen. Are you ready for the next door then?"

"Well, okay, but can I just ask one thing first?"

"Certainly."

"I have no idea how I went to sleep on the waterbed and woke up here again. Are you *sure* I'm not dead? I think I can take it if I am."

The Firemaker laughed. "You're not dead, Helen, I assure you."

"Okay, thank you. Just checking. You do realize, though, that other than a few very fuzzy ideas, I can't make any sense out of what I saw behind the First Door. I mean, you get that, right?"

"It'll come to you, Helen. It takes time to absorb all this, but the learning behind each door is learning you must have, no matter what. You can do the work and acquire it now, or you can put it off and acquire it later. But you can't really move on in any significant way in your life without it."

"Move on? Move on to what?"

"Let me explain it this way. At the moment, your understanding of how life works is *frozen*, so to speak. Therefore, until you complete this course of learning, you can't go on to the next level, and your life will continue to look very much as it has in the past. Not a very satisfying thought, as I understand it."

"Not satisfying at all," I said.

The Firemaker continued, "Let me expand on that a bit. Not seeing more than you currently see is actually a *choice*. It's a choice not to do the work that would allow you to grow and understand so much more. You must *choose* to grow. In actuality, very little true understanding comes to us passively."

Instinctively, I knew she was right. I had to choose to understand more. It was elegantly simple.

If you're stuck, it's because you choose not to do the required work necessary to become *unstuck*. The onus rests squarely on our own heads and nowhere else.

"Okay, I do understand that. Well, I don't understand much about the Wheel, but I *do* understand about people having to choose to see more in order to grow. Thank you so much for explaining it to me, Firemaker."

She nodded and pointed to the next door. "Yes, Helen, of course. Are you ready for the next door, then?"

"Yes, Firemaker, I am."

The Firemaker led the way to the next door. On its tile was a painting of a pearl—perfectly round, white, and radiant—nestled in its oyster shell.

I leaned into the door, pushed it open and stepped through. The Firemaker followed, closing the door behind us as before. Then, from some hidden place, she produced the little slip of paper from my fortune cookie.

"You threw this away. May I suggest you hang onto it? You never know. It could come in handy."

"How's that?"

"Anything at all that happens on this journey may be worth a second look." The Firemaker paused for a moment, pointed over my shoulder, and said, "Now watch this."

I turned and was amazed, more like horrified, to see my image projected high up on an enormous movie screen. "Wha—what am I doing up there?"

"Just watch. Suspend your fears and disbelief and be as conscious as you can. Be especially aware of your conclusions. I'll rejoin you soon." I turned to ask another question, but The Firemaker had gone.

I looked back at the giant screen and watched spellbound as I saw myself slipping down corridors of the past, gathering up my pain and sadness. I saw how over the years, I gradually had become more comfortable with sadness than with joy, eventually almost forgetting there were any other ways to feel.

Sadness had become a sort of perverse inner companion, a symbol of my essence, or at least what I believed my essence to be.

Next, I saw my sadness transformed into an enchanted pearl. It hung from my neck, close to my heart, and, in some strange way I didn't comprehend; it made me feel different — special.

The Pearl of Sadness had been with me for so long, I could barely recall when it hadn't existed. The images on the screen soon showed me how it had been formed—much like the grit that invades the oyster—from the cold, hard knot that had settled into the center of my chest so many years ago in childhood.

I'd never known how to get rid of my sadness and the pain that caused it. Now, I could see the truth was that I might not have been willing to let go of it even if I'd known how. Sadness had become the only feeling I really trusted, the only feeling that let me know I was alive, especially when those black night terrors woke me up and I couldn't remember who or where I was.

Lost in thought, I quite abruptly became aware that I was not alone. I was suddenly standing in the balcony above an auditorium full of people, unseen by the hundreds who had come to speak about their pain and bear witness to the sins and failures of their past.

"I'm an alcoholic!" shouted one.

"I hear ya'," called out another. "I'm a survivor of child abuse!"

"Yeah, me too. And I'm an overeater on top of it!" someone yelled from the back of the hall.

"That's a rough one!" another joined in, "Me, I'm co-dependant!"

"I'm this!" and "I'm that!" the people cried out to each other.

In a flash of knowing I realized that, just like me, their illnesses and injuries had become the foundation of their lives. *They were naming themselves according to the particular wounds they had suffered!*

Instead of building on the things they loved that brought them joy, they'd built on sorrow and despair and now they found themselves living in the soggy landfills of their past.

One by one, they all came to the front of the auditorium, told their stories, claimed an identity, and were handed a Pearl. As they returned to their seats, Pearls in hand, they applauded and commiserated with one another, overjoyed at being recognized for their suffering and their courage. They were incredibly proud of their Pearls, and many wore more than one.

In the dim light of the hall, the Pearls glowed like snowflakes falling on a winter's night. Observing from the balcony, I saw the room was not unlike a sanctuary and the people were not unlike worshipers as they caressed each other's Pearls and prayed to their Gods of Pain.

My heart went out to them because I knew they really didn't understand what they were doing. I hadn't realized I was doing it *myself* until a few moments ago. Just like them, my life had been spent pretending I was looking forward when, in fact, I was always looking back.

It was clear to me now that the Pearl was a product of a person's struggle, nothing more than a smooth coating formed around an old irritation. We'd all forgotten that it was our ability to transform the grit of life into something manageable that was the treasure, not the Pearl that had been formed in the process.

Certainly the Pearl was a worthy symbol of all we had survived and endured. Certainly discovering what was wrong and righting it was important, very important, but it wasn't the place to stop. It was the place to *start*.

Suddenly, my heart ached for these people, and for myself, and for the tiny prizes we'd settled for instead of real growth.

As long as we confused who we were *as people* with these Pearls we had created and for which we had paid so dearly, we'd never understand that, deep inside, no matter what happened in the past, we were all right.

Without that understanding, we'd keep on searching endlessly for some external something to protect us, to make us feel okay, not realizing we were already able to protect ourselves, and that we were already okay. Our Pearls were simply proof of that process, not the process itself, much less a final resting point.

I couldn't stand it anymore and screamed out, "It's a mistake to confuse what happens *to us* with who we *are*! We are so much more than that! SNAP OUT OF IT!" But nobody batted an eye. They were all completely oblivious to any sound I made.

It took a few moments to get my emotions under control and try to accept that they couldn't hear me — or wouldn't hear me. Slowly, it dawned on me that they weren't ready to leave. I shrugged my shoulders sadly, turned and headed for the nearest exit.

Pushing it open, I walked back into The Garden. The sun was just coming up, and the sky, once again, was orange. I yawned and stretched, then climbed into the hammock hanging beneath Aunt Betty's branches. And as I did, the slip of paper from the fortune cookie fell out of my pocket.

I leaned down, picked it up and held it once more to the light. Now it read:

YOU ARE THE CREATOR, NOT THE PEARL

SEVEN DOORS OF THE FIREMAKER

CHAPTER 11

MISTS

After the Second Door, I slept very soundly and awoke thinking, "The Firemaker told me this was the place for change and it's that for sure."

I sat up and swung my legs over the side of the hammock. Just then, I saw The Firemaker walking toward me on the path, about twenty or thirty yards away.

She called out, "Have a nice sleep, Helen?"

"Yes. I feel great, all clear and refreshed."

The Firemaker nodded. "Excellent. Any thoughts on your journey so far?

"Oh yes. I think the Second Door was about self-fulfilling prophecies. At least, part of it was.

"It seems like everybody in that auditorium was sort of *willing* himself or herself to a life of being stuck. That's not a very scientific take on it on my part, I know, but that's what it looked like to me."

"I see. Any insights about that regarding your own life?"

"In some ways, that *is* the story of my life. And it's the story of a lot of other people I know. We get stuck, can't seem to move forward.

"Then, something comes along and propels us from wherever we are to the next place, and usually against our will. That's a pretty rough way to get moved along. I don't understand why it works that way. Can you tell me?"

"Of course. Remember I said before that, as you are passing through the doors, you should be very conscious of your conclusions?"

"Oh yes, I remember. Your point was that often we need to stand back from ourselves a bit and really *watch* what we're deciding."

"Correct. Now I'll add a second point as well. Be sure you leave room to imagine the possibility of *good* in what you see in the Land Behind the Doors, even if something appears to be negative at first.

"It does no good to judge yourself, the people in the Auditorium, or the people at the Wheel too harshly. First of all, you may not be seeing all there is to see because of preconceived attitudes and notions. And preconceptions can color your conclusions."

"What do you mean?"

"At the Wheel, did you notice the woman spinning for a new kidney for her friend, or the doctor from Africa spinning for more help and medicine for his little bush hospital?

"In the Auditorium, did you see the gentleman who brought his daughter in order to demonstrate the depth of his remorse for having hurt her with his drinking, or the young woman who wrote in her journal, 'I am free to choose what I do, and who I will be.' Did you notice any of that?"

I frantically searched my memory. "No, Firemaker. I didn't see them at all. Are you sure they were even there?"

"Oh yes, they were there. And that's the problem with prejudging a situation. Because of old and ingrained preconceptions, you *thought* you understood. Everyone you noticed *seemed* to be greedy or foolish or stuck.

"But here's the key point, the one you must grasp: It's an infinite universe, Helen. No one understands anything *completely*, at least not on the levels at which human beings presently exist.

"What you saw at the Wheel and in the Auditorium *was*, on the surface at least, disturbing. But consider this: isn't it better for a person to do whatever she must to begin healing than to deny she has a problem at all?"

"Yes, of course it is," I said, nodding my head in agreement. "They were probably all doing and saying the best things they knew to do and say to start getting better. Obviously, I'm the one who's stupid."

The Firemaker laughed.

"You're not stupid, Helen, far from it. You simply viewed the situation from the level at which you were in that moment.

"Helen, sometimes it might not look like it, but almost all of the time people are doing their best. Often circumstances make it extremely difficult for anyone, especially the person that is experiencing it,

77

to know with any real certainty what's actually happening.

"The people in the Auditorium were in the process of figuring out what meaning to attach to certain events in their lives, and at the best of times, it's no small task to do that, to write the *true* story of one's Pearls.

"Many of the people you saw may not have been moving all that rapidly, but there are reasons for that. One of the most important reasons is that we often make our choices while blinded by what are called the *Mists of Circumstance*."

"The Mists of Circumstance? I've never head of that. What exactly does that mean?"

"The Mists of Circumstance are made up of events, relationships and attitudes that combine to obscure our vision. It's as if we're looking through the fog at night, and this makes it nearly impossible to know with any certainty in advance whether our choices are good ones.

"So, what happens is that shortly after making a decision, if things don't go immediately the way we'd hoped, we tend to look back and think that we were wrong. It's a common thing to do. But as time passes and our vision clears, we often see we made the right choice."

I thought about that for a while. "You know, you're right. I look back at my decisions all the time and I almost always decide I blew it. But once in a while, way down the road, I realize that I *did* make the right choice after all. Unfortunately, the problem seems to be, Firemaker, that until you know that's true, the doubts just keep on coming."

"Yes, certainly. But as you move through the remaining doors, the Mists will begin to fall away and you'll see the correct choice in advance more and more clearly.

"Until then, simply knowing that the Mists *exist* and allowing for the difficulty of seeing through them will lessen your anxiety. And just as important, knowing this will free you from the heavy weight of judging others.

"Just like you, the people in the Auditorium fear that some choices made recently or even long ago have ruined their lives. But to judge that choice without taking into consideration the Mists of Circumstance is to see only a very small part of the larger whole.

"It's a point of view that condemns any choice that was less than one hundred percent perfect, and that's an impossible standard.

"So, the next time you find yourself drawing somewhat hasty conclusions about a person's behavior, especially your own, consider the hidden reasons behind such a choice, reasons you probably can't see, like pain or illness or fear. Those are the Mists of Circumstance and every other person's will surely be entirely different from yours.

"Someone may be struggling with something you are unable to see, much less understand, because it's an experience you've never had or one that you cannot decipher.

"Here's something else to think about, and while it might be challenging to comprehend at first, in the end it may offer an interesting perspective.

"If someone in desperate emotional pain chooses to drink heavily rather than to commit suicide, *at least they're still alive.*

"That means they still have the opportunity to change available to them. They still have a chance to continue to grow past the heavy drinking.

"Isn't it better for a person, even if she's a hundred pounds overweight, to have another cookie than to give up on living? Because once the choice to give up is made, there can't be any other."

I nodded as I let this sink in. "I think I get what you're saying, but I'm confused about something. Don't people need limits? I mean, don't people overdo the handling of their pain by eating or taking drugs or driving their cars too fast, you know, anything that might help them escape it for a while?

"And what about going so far that you hurt somebody else? The kind of stuff you're talking about tends to get people into a lot of trouble.

"It seems to me that most of the people I saw in the Auditorium were there either because they, or someone close to them, had been doing too much of something negative in order to avoid pain in real time."

"Of course that's true. It only makes sense to recognize the potential for self-abuse born from such pain, and you're right to be concerned about the damage inflicted on others as a result of self-abuse, too.

"But what I'm talking about is someone in a truly desperate state of mind, a mind so filled with anguish it can't take another moment of pain, another moment of life. To turn to something else, even though that something else might eventually be the cause of more anguish, is still to choose life over death.

"I know that sounds paradoxical and runs counter to everything you've been told about being tough and resisting the temptation to self-medicate, but how many people were simply not tough enough to face another day without relief, even relief that comes from a questionable source? Are they better off dead?

"What I'm telling you is that, when a person chooses life, she chooses the *possibility* of growth and change and right action. The homeless panhandler you see passed out on the street today may save a child's life tomorrow.

"In every individual, *in each and every moment,* there exists the potential to become something greater, to evolve, to truly recover and to become whole. But all that is negated if the person chooses death."

The Firemaker paused to let her words sink in. "Let me tell you a little story, Helen. I think you'll find it interesting and quite educational."

SEVEN DOORS OF THE FIREMAKER

CHAPTER 12

THE CITY OF JOY

"As the story begins, you and some friends have just learned that a place called the City of Joy exists somewhere out there beyond the horizon. It's a place of peace, happiness and beauty.

"You all talk it over and, in time, put together a caravan and set out to find that marvelous place. Why wouldn't you? It would be madness *not* to want to live in such a place.

"So, your provisions are gathered, maps are obtained, transportation is arranged and you set out. At first, things go very well and everyone is in great spirits.

"But along the way, you quite unexpectedly enter a place called the Terrible Desert. None of the maps showed this challenging place, so you're all entirely unprepared.

"In the Terrible Desert, you're assaulted by bandits and hammered by sandstorms. There's no fresh water, and you think you'll die from the sweltering heat. Soon, the caravan comes to a complete stop. You're stuck. Stranded.

"Weeks pass with scant food, water and shelter, and you despair of ever getting out alive, much less of finding the City of Joy. In fact, the City of Joy is the last thing on your mind. You just want out of this terrible place and into any place that's better.

"Fortunately, just in time, another caravan comes along, heading for a place of safety. These travelers were once in exactly the same straits as you, but somehow they managed to make it out, get back on their feet, and find a decent, safe place to call home, the City of Stability.

"Because they learned many a hard lesson before and took it to heart, they're now able to pass through the Terrible Desert safely. They know what to look out for in themselves and the environment. They know where the water is, where the bandits hide and where the quicksand lies.

"And, they know that as long as certain rules are adhered to and the path that got them out before is followed, the odds are very good they'll never be stranded in the Terrible Desert again."

"I think I'm starting to get it."

"Good," said The Firemaker. "Now, let's say your caravan joins the caravan that knows the way to the City of Stability, and with some real effort and the help of those who have been there before, you all make it safely there. Naturally, you're relieved to be out of the madness, danger and despair. You're elated simply to be safe and fed and warm.

"Who does that remind you of, Helen?"

I nodded because it was so obvious. "Me in Peri's garden." Then I added, "And a lot of the people in the Auditorium?"

"Correct. So, to return to the story, of course you are ecstatic to be in the City of Stability. For a while, maybe for a *long* while, you're content to repeatedly discuss and relive the difficulties and challenges you overcame in the Terrible Desert. Recounting the horrors is comforting and a way to release the fears.

"It also helps you feel empowered when you re-member that it was once *very* bad and now it's much better. Even more important, it's wonderful to realize that you've stopped the blind wandering and that things are so much better largely because of your own intelligent efforts. It makes sense to gather together with others of similar experience and share all that."

"And that's what admiring each other's Pearls is all about."

"Correct again. And to judge that harshly is to deny people their joy, power and self-direction.

"Even so, there almost inevitably comes a time when you begin to long for *more* than stability. Stability is important, certainly, but it often doesn't nurture the parts of us that are the most inventive and alive. You find you miss being creative. But creativity isn't encouraged in the City of Stability.

"In fact, if you get too creative, the 'Old Masters' of Stability—those who've been there the longest and who've decided that where they are is good enough for *everyone*—may sternly warn you off becoming too bold. They may even tell you that you risk being thrust back into the Terrible Desert if you don't calm down and worship your hard-won Pearl like a good girl.

"But just being stable isn't why you were put on this earth. You weren't born just to put out negative fires and dwell on past victories. You're here to light new fires of creativity all your own. And that's the impulse, the drive that makes you begin to hunger once more for the City of Joy."

"Yes, I see. I'm beginning to understand a little of that, to long for that. But if I ache so much to move forward, then why am I still stuck in the City of Stability? In fact, why don't *all* of us get up off our rear ends and just go for it?"

"Many reasons, Helen. There's the fear of old disasters revisiting you and the fear of new demons you may not be able to recognize. There is a reluctance to let go of stale relationships and the fear of taking risks. And there are many, many more.

"But eventually, despite their fears, most people *will* press on toward the City of Joy. It is as inevitable an impulse as the one that birds feel in migration. It's built in to all of us to desire to grow, to rise, level by level, until we reach our final destination.

"And this journey you're on, traversing the Land Behind the Doors, means you've left the City of Stability and are again seeking the City of Joy, just like you sought the piece of sun as a little girl. The two pursuits are the same, and that's what you're doing right now."

As The Firemaker told the story, I began to understand more about myself and my experiences behind the Doors. It was as if something that had been all knotted up for a long time had gently begun to come untangled. But still there was something she said that puzzled me.

"Firemaker, what about the people who spend their *whole* lives stuck, doing the same things over and over and over again? I mean, why doesn't the Universe just kick us out of the Auditorium so we'll get on with it?"

The Firemaker laughed. "Well, Helen," she said, "in spite of what you may have been told, the Infinite Intelligence that created the Universe isn't the least bit concerned with how long you sit around in the Auditorium admiring your Pearls. Not the least bit."

"But how can that be?"

"Things are set up that way because what you want matters, especially to *you*. And the Universe respects that. You see, you have been set free on the path of exploration to exercise your Free Will. Otherwise, you'd be nothing more than a robot.

"Just know that sooner or later, no matter who you are, you will eventually sense that for maximum growth it would be far better to remove the Pearl, the negative past, all of it, from the center of your consciousness.

"Otherwise, you'll just keep building a bigger and bigger Pearl all your life. And there's such a thing as a Pearl that's become too heavy to carry, a Pearl that's too large to circumnavigate. In fact, circumnavigation is a good way to remember this lesson.

"Once, the idea that the world was *flat* was such a large and collective Pearl in human consciousness, that, for all intents and purposes, it *was* flat. For most of human history, nobody could circumnavigate such an enormous Pearl and begin to conceive of the idea that the world might be round and could be..."

"*Circumnavigated!* Yes, I understand! You're saying the Pearl is really a temporary stop, a way station along the greater journey of a person's life, or our collective lives as human beings, right?"

"Very good, Helen. And, because it is built into human beings to keep progressing, your own boredom or impatience with staying at the Pearl level will sooner or later put you back on the path, seeking to solve the greater problem."

"Which is..." I said slowly, "to pass on through the Auditorium dedicated to the Pearls of the Past and remove the Pearl from your life once and for all?"

"Exactly. And to do that, you have to move forward and smash the Pearl altogether. It is the only way to be rid of it and ultimately, nothing less will do.

"There's nothing sadder than the person who lives her life in the *good old days* and never moves on to the good *new* days based on who and what she is in the present."

"But Firemaker, I have no idea how to smash my Pearls."

"Not yet, but if you continue this journey, soon you will. Until then, I can tell you that since the pain goes *on* in layers, it must come *off* in layers too. That process must continue until the Pearl becomes a size that you can manage—and then you can smash it and be done with it once and for all."

The Firemaker paused. "But I think that's enough about Pearls and a flat earth for now. I realize it's a lot to absorb. And besides, I believe you are anxious to go through the next door."

As usual, it was all a bit overwhelming, but I wanted to go on, so I shook the dizziness from my head and with a smile, told her, "I'm ready."

SEVEN DOORS OF THE FIREMAKER

CHAPTER 13

THE THIRD DOOR: THE BEEHIVE

Outside the Third Door, I paused and looked carefully at the tile. It was a drawing by one of Peri's nieces, a honeybee circling a yellow daisy and, in the background, a beehive. After a moment, I pushed the door open and stepped through.

A little more than ten yards away was a lonesome tree stump with a bold, crudely painted sign nailed squarely to its bark. Cut down a long time ago, the remains of the tree had been put to use for travelers like me. The sign read:

KEEP GOING

Below the words an arrow pointed in the direction of a nearby dirt road. "All right, I'll bite," I said.

I took the road and walked for what felt like an hour or maybe a bit more. The road began to veer somewhat to the left, gradually becoming less defined and eventually turning into what looked like some kind of very old hunting trail or animal track.

I was tired, and not knowing where I was going wasn't helping my mood either. "Okay, Firemaker, what now? Can you hear me? I'm about out of road here. What do I do? I need a little input."

There was no response so I kept walking. Now the open, sunlit fields I'd been walking through melted away into a dense cover of thick trees that seemed to match the now-darkening sky.

Then, from not far ahead where the trail narrowed and the trees turned to even thicker woods, came a sound that at first I mistook for a buzz saw, more vibration than sound, really.

With great caution, I walked further down the trail toward the sound, until I discovered the source.

There, right in the middle of the path and blocking my way, was a giant beehive, seven or eight feet tall, and alive with swarming bees!

"Look at the size of that thing! How am I ever gonna get around that?"

Retreating a few steps, I climbed up on a nearby rock under the branches of an ancient Live Oak that looked an awful lot like Aunt Betty and leaned back to consider my options.

"One thing's for sure, I can't go ahead with the Mother of All Beehives sitting in the way. I could go back the way I came, I guess. Or I could try to go around the woods, but who knows how far it is or how long it'd take? And where am I going, anyway? For all I know, maybe I 'm already there."

Just then, I caught a swift movement out of the corner of my eye. A naked woman streaked down the trail past me, running toward the hive, crying, "I need, I need! I need the honey! I need it now!"

I nearly fell off the rock. I could see the woman was in for major trouble. Regaining my composure, I called out, "Lady! Wait! Are you nuts? There's a humongous beehive with a gazillion bees up ahead, and you're naked as a newborn! They'll sting you like crazy!"

But the woman, heedless of my warning and heedless of the bees, sped toward the hive, body exposed, arms outstretched, hands held high as if Santa Claus himself were up ahead.

As she passed, our eyes met for a split second and she yelled, "Mind your own business, you stupid cow!"

I couldn't watch anymore. I hunkered down, burying my face in my knees. "Oooh, man! This is gonna be nasty."

Sure enough, a couple of seconds later, here came the naked woman, running at top speed, screaming in pain trying to get away from the hive. She was covered with bees and hundreds more followed in hot pursuit.

I hid behind the tree so they wouldn't decide I was a juicy target too, and as she ran by, I could see she was in terrible agony.

She had a puzzled expression on her tortured face and called out, "Why do they hurt me like this?" She fled up the long path and was soon out of sight.

I just stood there with my mouth open, unable to utter a word.

A few more minutes passed. The Firemaker still hadn't appeared, and I still no idea what I should do. For the moment, though, that was all right with me because I needed a little time to get over what I had just seen.

Before I could completely recover from the shock, though, I saw another woman heading for the hive. This one sort of sauntered, with a slight swing to her hips and a jaunty toss of her head.

Her only clothing was a thin silk slip that she had accessorized with sunglasses, a jungle helmet, and a brightly colored scarf tied around her neck.

On her feet she wore knee-high rubber boots, and in her left hand she carried a red plastic sword. Every now and then, she thrust it into the air and twirled it around in wide, loopy circles. Off she went toward the beehive.

"Not another one!" I groaned. "Unbelievable!"

"Lady! LADY! Wait a second! There's a giant beehive up ahead. I just saw another woman…"

But just as before, this woman paid no attention. I tried several more times to get her to stop, but she shot straight to the hive.

"Shut up, you silly twit!" she yelled as she passed by.

A few seconds later, here she came again, running back the other way, screaming and swatting at the bees as they stung every exposed part of her body.

"Why do they hurt me like this?" she yelled at me, then vanished down the trail.

I dove behind the tree again for safety, dumbfounded by the unfathomable foolishness of what I'd seen. I stood there leaning against the tree for a long while, waiting for the sick feeling to go away.

Then, suddenly, it occurred to me that I didn't know and couldn't know, what those women were feeling that would cause them to behave that way. The Firemaker had cautioned me not to judge too quickly, and for once I was doing things right.

Perhaps these women were simply misguided, not stupid, as I first thought. Perhaps these women are wearing Pearls of pain so large that they were blinded to the dangers of the hive?

Just then, someone behind me spoke. "How are you doing there, little lady?"

Startled, I slowly peeked around the tree. "I—I'm fine, thank you. Who are you?"

"I'm the beekeeper. That's my hive down the road there." The beekeeper was covered from head to toe in a suit that protected her whole body. In her right hand, she carried an iron pot. White smoke poured out of it, swirling around her like a halo.

"My name's Helen," I said, walking around the beekeeper to look at her equipment. "Isn't your suit uncomfortable?"

She laughed, "Not nearly as uncomfortable as a few hundred bee stings. Anyway, I've been at this so long I hardly notice the suit anymore. Wouldn't go near the hive without it."

"Well, I've been sitting here watching people go buck naked and half naked over to the hive like it was a darned tea party or something. I tried to warn them but they went ahead anyway. Unbelievable."

The beekeeper snorted, "I see it all the time. Just about nobody wants to listen anymore. There's no point trying to get people to protect themselves if they just won't listen. Have you ever been stung?"

I nodded. "Several times. It's sure not a very nice experience."

"Nope. And unlike a lot of things that toughen you up, this only gets worse. No immunity from it if it happens too often. After awhile, if you've been stung often enough, it only takes one sting to make you really sick.

"It's like an allergy, you know? You become allergic to the poison and when that happens, well, one sting is as strong as a hundred. It even kills some folks."

"So I've heard."

"Yep. But you can't blame it on the bees. They make honey and they sting. That's just a part of what bees do. People want the honey and they think they can just ignore the stings. Never works." She shook her head sadly. "Nope, never works.

"Well, I gotta get to work here. You take care of yourself now, Helen."

"Wait! Can you tell me how I can get past the beehive so I can keep going?" I called to her as she walked toward the bees.

"Getcha a suit!" she called back over her shoulder without stopping.

"But where — how do I — ?"

Too late. The beekeeper was on the other side of the hive, already deep into her work. My words just hung in the air, fading into the buzzing of the bees. "Great. Now what do I do?"

Suddenly, and for no reason I could put my finger on, I remembered my pouch. Lifting the string from my neck, I quickly opened it and reached in for what I hoped would be the promised bit of good luck.

I pulled out a gold coin, plain except for this one simple word inscribed on its face:

INSIDE

More bewildered than disappointed, I turned it over, curious about what was written on the other side. It read:

BELIEF PLUS ACTION IS THE SUPREME LAW OF LIFE

"What the heck does that mean?" Frustrated, tired, dazed, and still queasy from what I'd seen, I could only stand there and look at the coin, reading the words over and over again.

Finally, I pulled myself together, stuck the coin back in the pouch, put the string around my neck, and stood up.

"Well, this is getting me nowhere. Clearly the only choice is to backtrack." I started out the way I'd gone in, walking slowly, glad to leave the sound of the hive behind me.

As I walked, the words kept ringing in my ears: *"Belief plus action is the Supreme Law of Life."* Over and over it played, like a broken record.

And, because I already felt so unsettled about what I had seen the women at the Beehive doing, the singsong going on in my head made me feel even worse.

"Fine! *Belief plus action is the Supreme Law of Life!!!* I get it already. Well how about this? I BELIEVE I WANT OUT OF HERE RIGHT NOW, AND I MEAN IT!"

In the heat of the moment I grabbed a large stone and bonked it against a tree — *ka-thunk!*

"How's *that* for action?" I yelled even though I knew what I was doing made no sense.

As I stepped back, I lost my balance, stumbled backward into a large bush, tumbled over and landed on my bottom.

CHAPTER 14

THE PEOPLE IN THE BEEHIVE

When I looked up, I was somehow, magically in The Garden again sitting under the sheltering branches of Aunt Betty. The Firemaker was standing only a few feet away, having a nice laugh.

"That was nice work, Helen. You're starting to get the hang of all this. I'm proud of you."

I got up, rubbing my butt and picking twigs out of my hair. "But I didn't do anything except have a tantrum, throw a rock and fall down."

"Well, in truth you'll rarely know *exactly which* action was the key that unlocked what you wanted. Sometimes you have to make a lot of noise and thunder like you just did to get the attention of a helper — such as myself.

"I helped you out a little bit on that one because you'd spent enough time at the Beehive. It was time for us to discuss your observations and for you to move on to the next door.

"But you typically won't get results like that so quickly and easily most of the time, at least not at first.

"Still, in essence you had the main ingredients for making the Supreme Law work. You said what you wanted and sincerely meant it, and you took an action, even if it didn't seem directly related to what you wanted."

"That's true, but I've said things and meant it before, and taken some kind of action and I didn't instantly get them."

"As I said, you will rarely know exactly *what* you did that triggered the response you wanted. The point is to go on believing and keep adding to the stack of actions you're building. Just know that, at this level, you are in direct contact with me and can ask for help, and you are gaining more and more power on your own.

"In this situation, you suspended judgment, demanded a way out, and I helped you get it in order to illustrate the Supreme Law for you. This was a minor demand and of little overall consequence to your life, and it was easy to assist you.

"But if it had been something that ran against your greatest good, I could not have helped you. Clearly that wasn't the case here.

"You haven't mastered the process, and you'll have plenty of misfires, but you're on your way. Now tell me, how did you find the experience of the Third Door?"

"It seemed like a real dead end, no pun intended. Complete and utter madness. There was a naked woman, a half-naked woman, a giant beehive, and a woman in a protective suit.

"I'm completely confused. Can you help me to see what it all meant because I sure don't know?"

The Firemaker said gently, "Tell me a bit about your family, Helen."

"My family? Hmmm. Well, there's nothing much to tell. I have virtually no contact with any of them and haven't for many years. Why do you ask?"

"Do you miss them?"

"Well, yes and no. I've always wished we had a loving relationship and could just be together sometimes without all the fighting, jealousy and anger that were there when I was living at home."

"So you long for the sweetness, the *idea* of family, yet you never call or visit them. Correct?"

"Oh, I've gone by my parents' house a time or two over the years when my brothers were all there for Thanksgiving or something.

"But it's always the same as it ever was. Nastiness breaks out and ruins everything. So, what you said is essentially correct—I never call or visit them."

"So focus in on that. Exactly *why* do you keep your distance?"

"It's just too painful. I always get hurt around them. I always feel like I'm in danger."

"So what was this door about, Helen?"

"I don't have the faintest—wait a minute! My *family* is the Beehive?"

"Yes, as is any relationship, addiction or habit that repeatedly hurts you. You tell yourself there's something sweet in there, but something stronger warns you that the price is too high or perhaps the sweetness isn't really there at all.

"The Beehive represents *any* connection you have that damages you again and again. It could be your family, a job, a lover, a friend, but the principle is the same. Do you see?"

I must have turned a little green or something because The Firemaker asked me how I was feeling.

"A little light headed, maybe."

"Is that the feeling you had as you watched the women go toward the hive?"

"Yeah, I felt sick all over."

"Like you'd been stung?"

"Me? Well, nothing happened to me. They were the ones who got hurt."

"Yes, they went in believing they could change the nature of the situation, or at least that they had it figured out, and they got stung. But look at how you're feeling from the experience now. Though indirectly, you were stung, too, Helen.

"What you were trying to do was keep them from doing something incredibly foolish and dangerous, but their reaction essentially was, '*How dare you try to keep me from getting stung? I'll sting YOU for that!*' And they did so, verbally.

"And if you had told them that they had hurt you with their words, it's very likely that they'd have stung you *again* for even suggesting that they sting other people with their words and actions.

"Yes, they stung you all right and that's why you feel so ill now. This is not sitting in *judgement* of their actions, only observing them so that we can discuss the impact of those actions upon you. "

"You're right, Firemaker. I thought I felt bad just because it hurt to see *them* hurt. But it was more than that. I was physically ill, dizzy and sick to my stomach. I had to put my head down and rest."

"Yes, being stung is much more than merely an unnerving experience. It's painful and disorienting and, as the beekeeper told you, it never gets any less so, no matter how many times it happens."

My brain was fast approaching overload. My whole notion of those women as victims and of myself as a victim had just been turned upside down.

Sure, they were injured at the hive, just as I'd been bruised and battered every time I attempted to go back to those dangerous places I thought held the sweetness I craved so badly.

But if I understood The Firemaker correctly, that was only part of the lesson of this door. There was also the lesson that those women—and all of us—do plenty of stinging too, and without even knowing it.

"So you're saying that we're virtually ALL *Stingers* in one way or another, *right?*"

The Firemaker answered, "Not all. Not people who have become aware of these concepts and have incorporated them into their lives.

"What I *am* saying is that if one is not careful, it's very easy to sting other people out of some misguided sense of self-defense.

"Being defensive and hurtful when *anyone* tries to help by suggesting an alternative way of behaving, is simply to choose a path that will result in lost ground in one's progress."

"Okay, I see that. But there must be a way out of this madness. If *belief plus action is the Supreme Law of Life* and all that, then what I believe and how I act in relation to the situation determines how it comes out, right?"

"Not entirely, but it's close to correct within the boundaries of your understanding at this moment. A few doors from now you will understand much more about how the law functions.

"But for now, your interpretation will suffice. Just understand that it's a guiding force for all human beings, whether they know it or not."

"What about this? In a Beehive situation, I believe two things: one, that there's sweetness in the hive that I long for, and two, that it's not worth getting hurt over."

"Yes, that's how it seems, but part one, thinking that there is sweetness in the hive, isn't your genuine belief. Your genuine belief is that no sweetness exists there, and even if there *were*, part two *is* a genuine belief: the price is too high.

"And that's how your life actually is. You don't have contact with the Beehive, your family, because you don't truly believe that sweetness exists there. As a result, you've concluded that abstinence from them is the only safe way to proceed."

"But what about those women who got stung, Firemaker? Didn't they believe in what they were doing? They certainly *looked* like it going in. Why did it end up so very badly for them if they were so sure of themselves?"

"In spite of appearances, deep inside, where their true beliefs reside, they knew what they were in for. But they overrode those beliefs and past experiences at the Beehive because they simply would not accept that bees have two natures that are involved, one to produce sweetness and one to sting, so they paid the price for ignoring one of those facts.

In most cases, people know that they're Stingers, as you call them, too, in spite of what they tell themselves to the contrary. The most effective way to keep your myths alive is to surround yourself with other people whose beliefs and actions are based on those same myths.

"Stingers don't look like Stingers to other Stingers. Or at least their behavior doesn't seem out of the ordinary or offensive and dangerous to other people who are using the same tactics.

"But back to *belief plus action*. You've seen films of beekeepers completely covered by bees and yet they're not stung. Why do you think that happens?"

"I guess it's because they aren't *pretending* that the bees won't sting them. Somehow they've learned how to go near the bees or even be covered in them and not get stung. And since they actually *know* it and *believe* it, that's how it comes out."

"Excellent, Helen. That's it exactly."

"Okay, I'm good with that then. But Firemaker, can you tell me who those women were? I felt like I knew them intimately somehow. The same feeling was true of the beekeeper."

"They were all versions of you during different phases of your life.

"The first woman was you, naked and innocent, full of need, blindly rushing in.

"The second was you, too, but a bit smarter, a bit more aware of the problems, yet still attacking the problem with the wrong tools. In that particular case, the tool was a toy sword.

"Finally, the beekeeper represented you when you are completely protected and full of knowing about the dual nature of the bees, or in this case, your own family."

"Ah, yes. Now I get it. Bees may make honey, but they also sting. So, either stay away from the hive or tell yourself the truth and be fully protected before you go in. Right?"

"Right. And?"

"And there may or may not be honey there in the first place."

"And?"

"Let me see. I'll bet I could find the honey or something just as tasty somewhere else without going through all that agony. I could go where there's honey readily available but with no bees and no hive. No beekeeper's suit needed.

"And, best of all, no stings, not by anyone, me included. But where do I find such a place?"

"The coin, Helen, think of the coin."

My mind flashed to the memory of pulling the gold coin from the pouch.

"Inside," I whispered, "Inside."

CHAPTER 15

THE FOURTH DOOR: THE DINER

The Firemaker nodded, "Yes, Helen. *Inside*. All the sweetness of life, all you could ever imagine or want, is right inside you."

"But it's not how I *feel*, Firemaker. I just don't feel all sweet inside."

"Not yet. You're still carrying a burden that must be put down first. Those sad feelings aren't really at your center. It's a trick of your ego, like a bad map that keeps leading you astray.

"But you're learning, and you'll find your way if you just keep opening new doors. Are you ready to continue, or do you need to rest?"

"No more rest, Firemaker. I've had it with rest. I want what's mine. I want *me*, free and clear, happy and sweet and full of love. I can have that, can't I? That's what this is all about, isn't it?"

"Yes, Helen, all that's true. Ready for the next door, then?"

"To the next door. Let's do it."

The Firemaker motioned to the Fourth Door. Its tile had been painted with the picture of a piece of pie. I smiled. There was no quitting now. I leaned my weight into the door, pushing it open with my shoulder. "I can do this. I can get through every last door."

The door gave way easily. With a whoosh and a stumble, I found myself standing just inside the entrance to an old-fashioned, Fifties-style diner. A revolving door was at my back and, tucked up against both sides of the long narrow room, twin rows of plump cherry red booths beckoned me to come in.

I looked around for a few seconds, found the closest empty booth and plopped down. Without asking if I wanted anything, a waitress slid up next to the booth, turned the white coffee cup upright and said, "Take cream with your coffee, honey?"

"Sure. Um, well, actually, do you have hot chocolate?" I asked, too late. My cup was already filled to the brim with coffee.

"Be right back with a menu, kid," she said, as she darted away, gliding into the kitchen on slick linoleum floors.

Almost as suddenly as she'd gone, she was back, flopping a menu down in front of me. I ordered a piece of banana cream pie as she pushed a dish full of those little plastic pots of cream over to me. You know the kind. Those little white buckets with flat, peel-off lids found in every inexpensive diner and café in the world? Right, those.

It wasn't long before I knew what this door was going to be about. The waitress grinned and got right to the point, "Ever had any of that boyfriend trouble, honey?"

"Oh, that. Yeah, I sure have. A truckload. Does it show?" I mumbled.

"Well, it's always that or money. Most everybody who passes through here's got problems with one or the other."

A smile sent her weathered face into a thousand lines as she darted away to fetch my pie and I called out, "Excuse me, could you make that *two* pieces of pie, please?"

"Sure thing, honey!"

She was back in a flash and we took up the conversation as if she'd never left.

"I guess you know all about bad relationships then," I said, digging into my first piece of pie.

"More than a little, honey, more than a little. Why don't you tell me your version?"

"The standard cliché. My relationships have been pretty disappointing, to understate it by a million percent. They're hypnotic and full of fireworks in the beginning, but in the end they always die some painful death. And unless I'm completely to blame every single time, I couldn't tell you why."

The waitress pushed the dish with the pots of cream closer to me, but kept listening without comment.

"It's funny you bring this up because I'd kind of just shoved *that* challenge onto the back burner. But when I think about it, boy, what a mess. No sooner am I out of one relationship than I forget how uncomfortable it was and get all itchy to be back in one again."

"That's understandable. Romantic love: Sweet as honey, but sometimes as dangerous as a swarm of bees, right?"

"Oh, so you know about the Beehive and all of that?" I asked.

Before she could answer, a flurry of swearing came from the kitchen. Flashing me a quick smile, the waitress hollered back, "You'd better not be fryin' those eggs back there, Charlie. And don't bark back at me, either! I told you the customer wants 'em soft boiled. It's not my fault nobody wants fried eggs and ham any more."

"Charley is old fashioned. Only way he knows to cook is to drop the food in hot grease and stand back until it catches fire." She casually rested her right hand against the tabletop and grinned at me again, as if exchanging insults with the cook was as much a part of her day as putting on makeup.

"About the Beehive, yeah, I know about that. I work in the Land Behind the Doors, kiddo. You pick things up."

"I guess so," I said, a bit uncertainly. "I really hadn't thought about it until now. But that Third Door wasn't just about family, it had a lot to tell me about my love relationships, too."

I swallowed another mouthful of banana cream pie. "You know," I said, "I really try to make these things work, and that's the honest truth. But something always goes wrong, and one of us becomes unhappy, and then soon we're *both* unhappy, and then we're finished."

"Sometimes being a couple ain't all it's cracked up to be. Mind if I sit? I'm on my break."

110

Without waiting for an answer, she slid into the seat across from me. "Look here, I'll show you something that might help. See these, whatever you call them, these little pots of cream?" She held up one of the small plastic cream containers.

"Imagine that one of these pots of cream is a person." She set the little bucket down on its base.

"Now, take another pot from the dish and stand it on its little flat head on top of that first one. Follow me, honey?"

I did as she said and stacked the two containers, top-to-top with one right side up and the other upside down. "Like this?"

"That's it. See, when you put them together the stack looks almost solid, right?"

I nodded.

"From the outside, it pretty much looks like one thing, one whole unit, doesn't it? And if you got real used to seeing the pots of cream linked up like that, pretty soon you'd think they came that way, like that's how they're supposed to look. You'd begin to think that one pot of cream alone is only half of what it ought to be."

"Uh-huh, I get it."

"Well, most people don't get that, at least not at first, if they ever do. And that's the problem. The individuals in relationships can become like these two pots of cream.

"From the outside they look like one unit, and all the single pots of cream, the single people, are so busy thinking how wonderful the joined-up units have it that they don't notice that one pot is sitting on top of the other.

"All kinds of unpleasant stuff can happen in a situation like that. I mean when you've got two people getting together just so they won't feel like they're incomplete."

I nodded. "I can definitely relate to that."

"So like most people, you fight with your boy-friends from time to time, I imagine?"

"Oh, certainly. More with some than I do with others. There were at least a few I wish I'd never met. It's a funny thing, but most of them turned out to be versions of the same guy over and over again, only with a different face, different body, and a different set of circumstances. It's almost as if they were series of *prototypes*. In fact I call the bunch of them my *Protos*. It simplifies things."

The waitress grinned, then laughed out loud. "*Protos* huh? I kinda like that!"

I nodded and continued. "Don't get me wrong, though, I'm not saying they were bad people or any-thing; there were some I really cared for, you know? I even came close a couple of times to finding that permanent sweet spot everybody longs for, but it never stayed sweet long enough."

By this time, even though I'm not a coffee drinker, I'd emptied a packet of sugar and a couple of those little gizmos of cream into my cup and drained it, and scarfed down all of the first piece of pie. Now I started on the other one.

"Like I was saying, it wasn't all bad, being with the guys I've been with. I wouldn't want you to think that," I said.

"I learned something about myself each time, about what I wanted and all. And there were good times, laughs and hugs and lovemaking along the way, too. Anyway, it's in the past, and what can you do? I'm over it, more or less.

"Except for *one* Proto. Gawwwd, I was crazy about him. And he was a handful, darned nearly the end of me. Probably thought the same thing about me, too."

I finished the pie, pushed my empty plate away and said, "Just like the others, it went sour right before my very eyes. Suddenly we were done, and I was in the revolving door again. It took me a long time to accept that he wasn't coming back,"

Now I was on a roll. The caffeine, the sugar, the sweet pie and the talk about love gone wrong had seriously loosened my tongue. Before I was finished I'd slogged through two more cups of coffee and my entire Rolodex of lost loves, near misses and absolute screw-ups.

"I should be wearing a tee shirt," I groaned, rubbing my too-full belly, "with a big broken heart on it that says, 'Unlucky in Proto Land' in fat red letters."

That was meant to be funny, but for some reason, the image of that sad tee shirt made my eyes well up with tears.

"Here," the waitress said, pulling a yellow handkerchief from her sleeve.

I dabbed my eyes and wrapped it up with, "You know, once it's all over, the reasons don't seem so important. But I still remember the way it felt when things started to go wrong.

"It's as if I was *compelled* to defend myself against something in the relationship, even if I didn't know what it was. I felt that if I didn't stand up for myself, what *I* wanted was going to go the way of the dinosaur, just vanish altogether."

"That's okay kid. We've all got our own love lament.

"But I'll tell you this much, what you're describing, that nagging feeling you couldn't put your finger on, well, that's what happens when you get into one of those stacked-up relationships. Shoot, girl it's usually not even personal. It's really about logistics.

"The one on the bottom struggles to get on top while the one on top struggles to stay there. It *shouldn't* be a battle for supremacy, of course. But once you're in a stacked-up deal, it's obviously a whole lot better to be the one on top than the one on the bottom. Well, unless the bottom is where you *want* to be." She squinted into the flame of her lighter as she lit up a cigarette.

"You know, even when it wasn't so bad, I always felt a kind of subtle jockeying for position going on, a kind of unspoken competition. Half the time I thought I was imagining it, or that something was wrong with me because I didn't know how to get along."

"Well, I don't know you personally, so I couldn't say if anything's wrong with you or not. Doesn't look like it from here. But what you're describing is how it is for lots of folks. Stacked up and messed up," she said, inhaling deeply.

She leaned back in the seat and flicked her long ash into the ashtray next to the napkin holder.

"And you've probably seen some stacked-up relationships where the same person always ends up getting hurt. You know, where the one on top stays on top and the one on the bottom stays on the bottom *all the time,* right? What a deal, huh? Be glad you're not in one of those."

"Oh, believe me, I am glad of that. But truthfully, that doesn't make me feel any better. I still want a partner in life. A good one."

"Well, don't give up, honey," the waitress said. She took the top pot of cream off the other one and placed it on the table, side-by-side with the first.

"It can also be like this," she said with surprising tenderness. "See, each pot of cream is already full but people just forget they're full and that in reality *nobody* else can fill them up. Getting that concept wrong is a fast way to ending up with another pot of cream sitting on your head."

I looked at the waitress and really studied her face for the first time. It was deeply lined with her living underneath the gaiety of her makeup. Clearly, she was speaking from experience.

She wore her hair in a beehive up-do and a small pink nameplate with "SUGAR" on it was pinned to her blouse. I smiled at the perfection of that name as a sudden burst of affection and familiarity welled up in me. It was as if I'd started every morning with breakfast in this diner and Sugar as my waitress my whole adult life.

"How rude of me. We've been talking all this time and I haven't even introduced myself. I'm Helen."

Sugar offered her hand and said, "I'm Sugar. I guess that's pretty obvious with this nametag on. Nice to meet you, Helen."

"Likewise," I said.

"Lemme show you something else, kiddo." Sugar pushed the two pots of cream together until they touched each other. "See that? Now that's a pretty thing. Each one is just exactly as important as the other, worth the same and holding the same amount of goodness.

"Being in a stacked-up relationship is worse than no relationship at all, if you ask me. But if you can get to *this* place, touching each other softly in this way, yet still equal at the base, then you've got something worthwhile.

"I know it can be hard to stop the cycle. After all, romantic love can work just like a drug. It makes you feel fantastic at first. But the high wears off and if things go bad, you're like a junkie without the fix. I think you get my point.

"The trick is, just try not to grab for romantic love like a life preserver every time the circumstances in your life change and you start feeling lonely or scared 'cause you think you're only half full."

CHAPTER 16

THE WHO'S-WHERE-IN-WHAT-ROOM CHA-CHA

Just then, several people met at the door to the diner with one group leaving as another group came in. They bunched up, facing each other and did that side-to-side thing where both sides guess wrong about which way the other is going and it looks like a kind of goofy little dance.

Finally, everybody laughed, sorted it out, and the "leavers" left and the "enterers" entered.

Sugar said, "That little cha-cha over at the door just now, you saw that, right? That group of folks going out and the other group coming in?"

"Sure, happens all the time," I said.

"Sure does, and in more ways than one. That's a good illustration of what we've been talking about. You meet people and hit it off for a while, things go great, then after a bit, you find them boring or in some cases, you can barely stand each other."

"Quite the mystery. What's behind that anyway, Sugar?"

"Well, it's like those people at the door just now. Some were coming into this room while others were just about to leave. But for a few moments, they were all in the *same* room, and their reasons for being in here at that moment were exactly the same: They came to get something to eat.

"Problem is, even though that interest was shared, and they probably could have had a nice chat about the food for a while, the people who were fed were already done with this diner, and the people coming *in* were just getting started."

"Whoa, I think I get it! You mean we're all in varying stages of doing whatever the room we're in is all about. If you're fed, the diner is something you no longer need, but if you're hungry, it's incredibly important to you."

"There you go, kiddo. For a little while you're all in the same room, and then you aren't. You could even extend it further to include the people who just sat down, the ones who've ordered, the ones who've been served, the ones who've eaten, the ones who've paid their bill, and the bunch we just saw, the ones exiting the room."

"Wow, that explains a lot, Sugar. People are at all sorts of different levels, busy experiencing what this particular room has to offer. They're all in the same room temporarily, but very few of them really notice how different *their* level is from the others around them."

"Right, Helen. They're all *diners* at the moment, and are still focused on the theme of this room, namely food, that's true. But at what *level of the dining experience* are they as diners?"

"I understand. Someone who just entered might stop and ask one of the people paying their bill how the food was, and that would be a common interest for a moment. But soon, the person who's leaving wants to leave. They obviously don't want to stay and chat about the food all the way through the other person's meal!"

I paused to think for a moment, then said, "So that's a big part of why so many relationships don't last. Somebody's just entering a room, and someone else has been there awhile but isn't quite done, and maybe there's somebody else who needs to move on right away. You could enter that room and not know the difference."

"Exactly," she said. "But it gets even more complicated because often the people in the room don't have any idea how much longer they're going to be there. Someone could be leaving the room tonight and not even know it."

"How in the world do you solve that problem, Sugar? It seems impossible."

Sugar smiled, "Not at all, honey. You just have to make sure that when you hook up with someone you take the time to see what they're about. And I mean *all* about. Nobody is about just one room.

"I'll give you an example. Let's say you meet someone at the art museum. Obviously you both like art or you wouldn't be there. But does that mean you'll like everything about that person? Hardly.

"You aren't going to spend your whole life in an art museum, but since lots of people consider themselves artists or lovers of the arts, they base their whole relationship on that one aspect, on that one room.

"It takes time and effort, of course, to find out about all the other rooms in a person's life, but it's essential. Remember, there are religious rooms, political rooms, sports rooms, bar rooms, you name it.

"And just because a person is in a room you like, that doesn't make it an automatic match. After all, is every Democrat the same as every other Democrat, or every Methodist exactly the same as every other Methodist? Of course not.

"So take your time going in, whether it's dating, a new friendship, a relationship at work, or whatever. Make sure one of you isn't leaving the room while the other is just stepping in. Or that you don't view the contents of the room so radically differently that it will become a source of problems later."

Sugar looked at the wall clock and gave me a little pat on the shoulder. "Well, my break is over. I'll see ya, honey," she said with a low, wheezy chuckle. She lit up another cigarette, took a drag, and started to dash away.

"Sugar?" I called. "Thank you."

She stopped, smiled, and waved away my thanks. "No big deal. Drop back in anytime. Banana cream pie is the dessert special on Wednesdays and in here, *every* day is Wednesday."

I got up then realized I didn't quite know what to do since I had no money with me. Sugar read my mind.

"Don't worry about the bill, kiddo. I'll put it on The Firemaker's tab," she said with a laugh. "Oh, and the next door? Just walk back out the way you came. You'll see. Bye-bye, honey."

Then, quick as could be, she was off serving coffee and counsel to another table.

I followed Sugar's directions, pushed against the revolving door, and stepped through it into The Garden. The Firemaker was there as always, quietly waiting.

SEVEN DOORS OF THE FIREMAKER

CHAPTER 17

THE GOOD, FLAT EARTH

"Hello, Helen. Did you have a nice snack at the Diner?"

"Yes, I did and you know, this last door got me to thinking. When it comes to relationships, maybe it's better not to count on things working out a certain way because they never seem to turn out the way I want them to. Or, for that matter, the way anybody else I know wants them to either."

"I take it you met Sugar."

"I sure did. She was amazing. Showed me a thing or two with those little pots of cream. I'm not exactly sure what conclusion you hoped I'd draw from that experience. But before Sugar explained things, I was feeling pretty sorry for myself, going on and on all about all my rotten Proto boyfriends.

"But like I was saying, even after all that Sugar showed me, or maybe because of it, I'm more convinced than ever that it's better not to get overly invested in specific outcomes. It's just a setup for all kinds of problems. Maybe that's not a very enlightened attitude, but what else can you do? You can't control anyone. You can't make anyone *get it*."

"Yes, it's important in life to give your expectations lots of room to breathe, Helen, because the Universe can give you much greater things than you can imagine.

"But it is also self-defeating to accept that things can go wrong and focus on that until it becomes an expectation.

"They're two quite different perspectives, with the first leaving the door open to wonder and surprise, and the second building in problems because of past negative experiences."

"Hmmm. Yes, I see the difference. I'll really have to watch out for that in myself in the future because I've sure done that second thing plenty of times in the past.

"Okay, if I may, I have another question that's not directly related to that."

"Certainly."

"Well, I understand about the search for this City of Joy place, Firemaker, but it doesn't explain how things work on a larger level, the level that explains what life is all about. And if I don't know what life is about, how can I work toward the outcome I want?

"I mean, even if I take the time in a relationship to make sure I'm not leaving a room as someone else is entering, and even if I allow my expectations lots of room to breathe, there's got to be more to the big picture than that. The Fourth Door certainly told me a lot about relationships, but that's only one piece of the puzzle.

"It seems to me that the way most of us live our lives is kind of insane. You know what I'm talking about, right? All the pain and darkness. I can't believe it was meant to be this way. Tell me Firemaker, how did it all go so wrong?"

"The truth is, Helen, it hasn't *all* gone so wrong.

"From space, even the largest cities on Earth are invisible to the naked eye. From there, the planet is perceived as a perfectly lovely blue ball and there is nothing dark or threatening about it.

"That may give you a sense of perspective. It's a good way for you to remember the enormity of the Cosmos.

"Of course, human activity is important, especially to humans. But in the grand scheme of things, it matters very little if human beings are behaving insanely for a while because that is a temporary aberration.

"Don't misunderstand; the madness you refer to can and does alter the progress of individual human souls, but my point here is that it can't alter Cosmic Order.

"No matter how it appears, everything is in balance even though at the level of your existence on the Earth plane it often seems quite the opposite.

"If that were not true, then a war, plane crash or an earthquake might set the whole Universe spinning out of control. But, as you can see, that is *not* how it works. Far from it."

I thought for a moment then said, "Okay, agreed, Firemaker, I get that. I do. But if *you're* the one who's injured or killed in one of those situations, or it happens to someone you love, your *personal* universe *does* spin out of control. That's true for sure," I said.

"Yes, on the personal level of course that's the case. And I'm not attempting to downplay the impact of such pain and trauma on human beings. As I said, such changes can and certainly do alter the progress of individual human souls. But they cannot alter Cosmic Law.

"If you could see it from a much higher plane, like an astronaut viewing the earth, you would see that even those events are in balance, as a part of the greater order.

"Things that you find undesirable don't exist at higher levels of consciousness. But they are *allowed* to exist at the level of human life at this stage of evolution because of the invaluable lessons they provide.

"One way to think of it is that human life, at this time, is like a driving school. Everyone alive at any given moment is learning how to operate and steer this intimately personal vehicle, the *Soul*, all on his or her own.

"Often, inexperienced drivers crash into each other, or an event that is required by Cosmic Order intervenes in individual lives. When that happens a collision may occur, and *that* can most definitely be terrifying."

She could see that I was still troubled.

"Let me give you this example: suppose you're watching a sweet, yellow butterfly sipping nectar from a flower. The sun is shining, the bees are buzzing and it's just a beautiful day in your life. That's a description of order, correct?"

I nodded. "Absolutely."

"But suddenly, a big blue jay swoops down and snatches the lovely little butterfly into its beak and gobbles it down right before your eyes. While it might be a shocking end to your idyllic scene of the previous moment, and fatal to the butterfly, does a bird eating a butterfly seem out of order? Does it seem as if suddenly everything in life has gone so wrong?"

"Well, no. That's just the nature of things. Birds eat butterflies, whether I like it or not."

"Correct, Helen. People kill other people, planes crash, and powerful hurricanes destroy lives and property, and on and on, whether humans like it or not. Because at this time in the evolution of the earth and its creatures..."

"That's just the nature of things, right?" I said.

"Yes. But that's not really what you're talking about. You're talking about how those kinds of things *feel* to you."

"Yes, that's it. I don't like it. I don't even like it that birds eat butterflies."

"I understand. But do you think that these things will be changing any time soon...wars and natural disasters and butterfly-eating birds?"

I didn't have to think long about that one. "No, I'm afraid not."

"Very well. Then right now, and I'm only talking about your existence at *this* level at *this* time, your task is not to understand all there is to understand about why Cosmic Order looks the way it does on the planet upon which you live.

"Rather, you must understand that what upsets you does so because *you want things to be different*. And that longing for things to be different is exactly what motivates you to grow and reach higher levels of consciousness. That is why you are on this journey right now.

"So there is *not* something inherently wrong in the cosmic sense. Buddha summed that up as: 'Life is suffering.'

"However, it might be easier for you to grasp if we edit that a bit to say: 'Life *includes* suffering.' And while you wish it didn't include suffering, on this plane at this time, it still does."

"Yes, Firemaker, but natural disasters and accidents are one thing. Wars and murder and all of that kind of mayhem are human creations and that's certainly not all right," I said.

The Firemaker nodded. "Helen, one of the main reasons many things are the way they are on Earth, both good and bad in your perception, is because of Free Will. We touched on this some time back, remember?"

"Yes, I do."

"Good. Now would be a good time to round out that discussion. Human beings are free to make their own choices about how they want to live, even if it is destructive to other human beings. That is where the knowledge that *belief plus action is the Supreme Law of Life* comes into play.

"If you don't believe it can be done, you're right. But on the other hand, if you think something is difficult but you still believe that you can do it, and you take action based upon that belief, often it happens exactly the way you want it to.

"That's what you did back at the Beehive when you believed so completely that you wanted out, and found your way out, with a little help from me."

"But what about when I exercise my Free Will and things go exactly the opposite of what I want?"

"That is simply a situation where your Free Will has been trumped by Cosmic Order. Life is a partnership between Free Will and Cosmic Order, a compromise between what you want and what *must be* in order to maintain balance in the Universe.

"Just because you choose a course and set out on it doesn't mean that you'll always arrive at the exact destination you picked. Sometimes you will and sometimes you won't.

"If there are other circumstances you didn't have knowledge of when you made your choice, some other events that *must* occur to keep things in universal balance, then your Free Will cannot counter that.

"But that doesn't mean it won't triumph in many, many situations. It will, and being here implies that you must do something with your Free Will.

"And yes, as you said, some people will use their Free Will to choose the path of destruction, and the human-made horrors of life will ensue. If you progress through seven doors, you will learn much more about people making such destructive choices.

"That learning, and the other teachings associated with it, will unlock many of the mysteries that have troubled you all of your life. But there is much work for you to do before you reach that point."

I thought about what she said for a minute. Thinking that I might be privileged to learn such important lessons made me tense and excited all at once. And I knew I wasn't ready. She surely was right about that.

"Yes, Firemaker, I understand, and I agree that I'm not ready for the teachings you're talking about yet. I know I'm still confused about a lot of things.

"But I have another question along those lines. Every religion that I'm aware of says there's a sacred and perfect system, a god-ruled system, for all of us to follow. According to them, we'll eventually end up in the City of Joy if we're good, or the Terrible Desert if we're bad, for all eternity. But all religions are *different* about how all of that happens.

"So in practice, on a daily level, at least as far as I can tell, no one *really* knows how anything works or how to get to the City of Joy for sure. How can any of us ever hope to grow past this if we don't know what we're doing or why we're doing it? I know it's a sign that I still have much more growing to do, but I *still* want the answer to the big WHY in the Sky, Firemaker!"

The Firemaker laughed. "Those are most ancient questions of the highest order. Religion is human-kind's system for addressing questions that do not have obvious answers unless one believes in invisible powers, often represented as a Supreme Being who cannot be seen or touched.

"Remember: *belief plus action is the Supreme Law of Life*. You have Free Will to believe as you want, and you may choose good or ill to believe in and act upon. But once you have made your choice and taken action on it, your whole world changes a little, or sometimes a lot, to fit your choice.

"That doesn't mean you can choose to have the Sun flicker out and it will happen. As I said, there is such a thing as Cosmic Order, and no one being can simply cancel that out with belief.

"But, you can choose what you will believe in and dedicate yourself to it and much of what you are after will come to you.

"So, your choice to believe in a Supreme Being or not is entirely yours, though people have argued for ages as to whether you can truly know that such a being exists. It's not my place to try and settle that debate here.

"What you *can* know, though, is that you're here, and since you're here you must *do something*. And yes, you can even choose to do nothing. But notice that 'doing nothing' still has the word *doing* in it.

"So, even if you choose to do absolutely nothing, what you're really doing is allowing your body's life force to ebb. Because of the nature of things, soon your earthly life will be gone and you won't be able to get it back. You only have so much time in this physical body."

"Okay, I think I understand. I'm here and even though I don't know *why* I'm here, practically nobody else does either. Therefore, I might as well just stop worrying about knowing the unknowable and get on with life, right?"

"Right. And?"

"And when I reach the appropriate level, more will be revealed. And if I decide to participate in a religion or not, I'm still functioning under the Supreme Law of Life. Namely, I'm choosing what to believe in and then acting upon that belief, right?"

The Firemaker nodded. "That's the point of being here, to get on with *your* life. The rest of it, 'the big WHY in the Sky,' as you put it, you'll know when you're ready, when you *need* to know in order to keep progressing, instead of just *wanting* to know.

"But that's enough about that for now because it's time for you to go through the next door. There is still much for you to learn."

Without another word, The Firemaker pointed to the Fifth Door. On the tile was a picture of a small loaf of bread.

I walked over, took a long, deep breath, stepped through the door, and was amazed to find myself on a quaint cobblestone street right out of a Dickens novel.

CHAPTER 18

THE FIFTH DOOR: THE BAKERY

It was snowing on the street and the quick change from the summer atmosphere of The Garden was an abrupt shock. Dressed only in my windbreaker, cotton blouse and jeans, I began to shiver.

Hands jammed into my pockets, I walked for several blocks, getting colder and colder, wishing I was wearing a heavy coat, until I finally came upon the storefront of a bakery. The smell of baking bread and the promise of warmth instantly made my decision for me and I stepped in.

Inside was a hubbub of activity, with all kinds of baked goods going in and out of the ovens at a brisk, steady pace.

At ground level, there was a short counter, about half the height it would normally be, with a low ceiling fan spinning above. The combination of the two features forced the customers to bend down to hand in their orders.

At that counter there was a kind of frantic air to the people's actions that reminded me of my experience at the Big Deal Wheel. Everyone seemed a bit jittery, uncertain and in a hurry.

A baker in her tall, white hat and white apron stood in the middle of things behind the counter, directing her helpers.

To the right, next to the front door of the bakery, a staircase ran up the wall and led to another counter. It stood on an open deck that formed the ceiling above the lower counter. Another baker stood behind it, managing things just as the baker on the lower level was doing.

The customers who chose that route all stood comfortably before their counter because it was of normal height and there was nothing hanging down from overhead. As I watched from below, they all calmly placed their orders and seemed to be in no hurry at all.

Despite the clear advantages of taking the stairs up to the more comfortable counter, for some reason most people chose the lower counter.

Strangely enough, the bakers didn't pay much attention to the customers at *either* counter. They seemed almost robotic in fact, and rarely said anything. They simply checked each person's order, then handed it to one of the helpers, who immediately gathered up the ingredients, mixed them together, and popped them into the oven.

Everyone seemed free to choose the counter they wanted, higher or lower. And, once their order had been placed, the people from both groups went into a little waiting room on their level that had a glass window looking out onto the ovens behind the counters. There they could watch their orders being prepared in warmth and comfort.

The people at the upstairs counter seemed utterly content to read a book or even leave the shop and let the baker do her work, happy to pick up their orders whenever they were ready.

But the majority of the customers on the lower level kept coming back to the counter and yelling out new ingredients. They did this even after the helpers had begun mixing, which forced the staff to stop and start over, again and again.

"More nuts," shouted one man. "Less yeast," said another, then they dashed back into the waiting room. Round and round the helpers went, trying to keep up with their demands. The baker, however, remained entirely neutral and unemotional. Nothing rattled her at all.

I was famished and, while there were two or three people in line at the higher counter at that moment, there was no one at the lower counter right then. I bent down to avoid the overhead fan and gave the baker my order.

"Raisin bread, please," I said and went out into the waiting room.

You know, though, it's a funny thing about waiting for what you want. I could see that the people at the higher counter who waited patiently for their orders always got what they wanted or something better. But the people at the lower counter, the ones who kept yelling in changes to their orders, never seemed happy with what *they* got.

Considering all I'd been through behind other doors, you'd think I would have known better than to do what I did next, but…nope.

With all the people milling around and chattering to no one in particular on the lower level, I found it impossible to wait patiently after I handed my order in.

One woman said, "Will I get what I ordered or is this place some kind of rip off?"

Another said, "How do I know this baker is any good? She's certainly not very friendly!"

By now you know that I've always had a very hard time with trust anyway, and in a few moments my doubts got the best of me. When the woman next to me ran in and changed her order to banana bread, I was sunk.

Mmmm. Banana bread! Why hadn't I ordered banana bread? You *also* know by now that I really like bananas, even more than raisins. That would have been a much better choice, I thought, sweeter, moister, all around tastier.

"I guess it must be okay to change your order," I thought. "Everyone down here is doing it. I mean, my gosh, I'm only human so I should be able to change my mind if I want to."

Suddenly, I couldn't stop myself. I ducked down under the ceiling fan, ran back to the lower counter and called out a new order.

"I've changed my mind!" I shouted. "Make mine banana bread!"

Content with my decision, I went back in the waiting room and settled down. That is, until a man sitting next to me got up, ran back in and changed his order to whole wheat.

I thought, "Whole wheat! That's what I want! It's so much healthier than sugary banana bread. Plus all that fiber! I think I'll make mine whole wheat, too. Heck, how about *organic* while I'm at it?"

And so I changed my order *again*.

And again. And again. And again.

By the time it was over, I must have changed my order fifteen times. And I'm sure you can guess what happened. Right. My order came back burnt to a crisp—a big, flat, salty brick. And instead of raisins, it was chock full of rocks with a stinky blackened banana peel sticking out of the top.

I was disgusted with myself and uncertain what to do, but my time in the Land Behind the Doors had taught me a thing or two: when in doubt, try to go back out the way you came in and if that fails, look for the nearest alternative exit. It can usually be found right under your nose.

I ditched the loathsome loaf, left the bakery by a back door I'd found, and walked right back into The Garden.

SEVEN DOORS OF THE FIREMAKER

CHAPTER 19

GREATER AND LESSER

The Firemaker was standing near the green hammock. "A little unpalatable, Helen?"

"Yeah, my order didn't exactly turn out to be the treat I'd hoped for."

"No, it didn't look like very tasty. But you learned something important that you'll never forget. The learning was the point, not the treat. The experiences of the Fifth Door were meant to teach you about the Greater and Lesser Selves."

"Greater and Lesser Selves?"

"Yes, Helen. The Lesser Self, as I think you're beginning to see, is a place where the majority of human beings spend most of their lifetime. Please understand there's no judgment in that statement. Every human being has a Lesser Self. It's just how people are made up."

"But you said there was a Greater Self, too. You mean there's another self in here somewhere?"

"Not literally. Ultimately everything about you is part of the same self. But it will be far easier at this moment to understand it if you temporarily think of the Greater and Lesser Selves as being separate.

"You see, the Greater Self is the intuition-guided, super-conscious self and the Lesser Self is part of the same being, but functioning at a much lower level. It is dependant on others, demanding, and uncertain of its direction.

"That's not a bad thing. All babies start off in that state because they are unable to take care of themselves physically and emotionally for a long time. The Lesser Self makes sure that the child's caregivers know when it wants or needs things.

"The Greater Self is always present, too. But it exists in a much finer, quieter, more secure state than the Lesser Self. It's present in *everyone* at birth, and its nature is so patient and subtle that it takes much guidance and dedicated work to realize it even exists.

And it takes even *more* guidance and dedicated work to let the Greater Self take charge of one's entire wellbeing.

"A good way to understand it is to think of the Lesser Self as a seed or tiny sprout, something that's in the process of *becoming* whatever its potential says it can be. The potential for it to grow into, say a giant redwood, is the Greater Self. And even the giant redwood was almost all potential once—just a tiny, fragile seed."

"Yes, I see, but what keeps us from just shooting up into our Greater Selves and being done with this slow-growing Lesser Self nonsense?"

"In Cosmic terms, human beings are the same, in essence, as a giant redwood. It takes a long time to grow into a fully integrated life form such as Peri or Virgie. And there is one final step in evolution above that, the *Unified Spirit*, but I'll come back to that in a bit. For now, let's think back to the Bakery so you'll fully understand this lesson.

"The part of the mind that helps the Greater and the lesser Selves attain what they desire is the sub-conscious mind—in this situation, represented by the Baker behind the counter.

"The subconscious mind is the *Facilitator*, work-ing on behalf of both states of being, the Greater and the Lesser Selves. It is neutral and has no will of its own.

"It does not judge. It does not understand humor or sarcasm or irony. It takes every demand—every order—that comes over the counter literally and acts on it immediately.

"Oh, of course! Now I get why there were two levels of counters in the Bakery.

"The bottom level was symbolic of the Lower Self. Everything was lower including the counter, the ceiling and the fan.

"So the people at that level, including me, were operating from our Lower Selves and, well, pretty much acting like impatient children.

"The upper level was symbolic of the Greater Self. There, the counter and all of that were at functional heights and the people who placed their orders were mature, courteous and patient. They were obviously operating from their Greater Selves. I get it"

"Yes, Helen. Once the Baker — the subconscious mind — has the order from either of the two Selves, it *must* attempt to fill it.

"But the order can only be filled if the demand is strong enough and held in consciousness as placed long enough for the order to be completely 'baked,' so to speak.

"When that happens, then the thing desired — or strongly feared for that matter — is focused into being. Eventually it comes out of the Baker's oven and into one's reality."

"And that's why my order came out so messed up and lousy. I kept changing the ingredients. And since the Baker doesn't argue, she just kept redoing it as ordered until I'd made a complete mess of it, right?"

"Exactly. I realize that you may have read or heard about this truth in many venues and thought it sounded like a lot of wishful thinking or nonsense. But simply because your reality doesn't *appear* to bear it out, that doesn't keep it from being the truth.

"Until it is explained and demonstrated for you, it *appears* as if life is just random happening after random happening and you are a victim of its whims. But that is not so.

"You are giving the Baker the orders all the time, whether you know it or not. It is how human beings create things as individuals and there is no other way to do it."

"I think I understand, Firemaker. The sole job of the subconscious mind, the Baker, is to be a facilitator. Its job is to get the order out, not to be a wishes and desires cop. It does whatever it can to assist in the creation of what is intensely focused upon by the Greater or the Lesser Self, right?"

"That's right. The Baker doesn't invent or edit the recipes. She simply reads them and acts upon them exactly as the individual customer hands them to her. She's neutral. *Completely* neutral.

"You see, most people think that the way they are right now, inhabiting the lesser, more Earthbound regions of the Self, is all there is to reality, or as you'd say, 'The System.' And for you to understand The System, it's important for you to grasp the nature of the Lesser Self.

"It might be helpful to think of the Lesser Self as an actual baby, and the only thing the baby knows is what it wants. You could say that wanting is its job. It constantly desires and needs. It is raw and demanding and has little or no comprehension of where it's going.

"Because it knows nothing other than itself, it believes that itself, as it is today, is all there is or can ever be. It's the essence of all that's still in need of assistance and guidance in human beings.

"The Lesser Self has the potential to grow, of course, just like the baby, but emotional and psychological growth don't come automatically, or even on any particular schedule. In fact, the growth of the Lesser Self has little to do with physical age. When you encounter someone living exclusively in the Lesser Self, he or she could be nine months or ninety years old."

The Firemaker paused. "If I'm going too fast, Helen, please let me know."

"It's a lot to take in all at once, but I'm with you. Really. It's fascinating and it explains so much about my own life. Please go on."

"Very well. As you've seen, the subconscious— the Facilitator or Baker—is designed only to accomplish specific tasks, and it also acts as a bridge between the Lesser and the Greater Selves. When the Lesser Self cries out wanting something, it's actually giving an order to the Baker to figure out how to obtain what it wants.

"Many people, and you're one of them now, know bits and pieces of information about the Lesser Self. But what most don't know, what you haven't known, is that the Greater Self will always try and protect you, always try to elevate your existence, while the Lesser Self is barely even aware that something greater could exist.

"The Greater Self is always with you, Helen, and it cares for you unconditionally, without judgment, hurry or frustration. And it has no specific vision of your future, it can see all the possibilities for you and is available to guide you toward becoming your highest and best self.

"That means it can't intervene in your life unless you are open to its guidance. You see, for it to step in without your permission, except during times of extreme danger such as a life-threatening crisis, isn't possible, because that would diminish your choices and negate your Free Will.

"When one is at the earlier levels of growth, the Greater Self is there, but it is mostly just observing because a person isn't open and listening to its help.

"Without an open invitation from you, it can't intervene in daily life except to nudge you quietly, or as I outlined before, give you a giant burst of warning intuition in a crisis. You must grow until you are aware of the Greater Self, then invite it to take over. Rest assured, it knows infinitely more than the Lesser Self.

"You've been preparing to invite your Greater Self in for a long time, Helen. Although you haven't been aware of it, it's always been available to you, helping in ways that don't interfere with your Free Will. When you've passed through seven doors, you'll know what it means to live life through the choices of the Greater Self.

"Now, I promised to come back to an explanation of the evolutionary stage that can occur with the union of the Lesser and Greater Selves and the subconscious. As I said, now and then, although not often on the Earth plane, both selves and the subconscious become fully integrated and function as one being—a *Unified Spirit*.

"I believe you know of some remarkable individuals who have achieved this state...the Buddha, Jesus, Sri Rama Krishna and others.

"Once a human being has managed to transform the heavy baggage of the Lesser Self into the power to release all control of his or her life to the Greater Self, he or she can then fully unite with the subconscious.

"At that point, another transformation takes place. Again, it's very rare on the Earth plane, but once it happens, that person becomes a Unified Spirit.

"For a Unified Spirit, there is no longer anything left to slow down its evolution. It doesn't *think*; it automatically *knows* what's desirable for itself and others, and what's not.

"Through many fits and starts, through much trial and error, the Unified Spirit has acquired the tools it needed to become whole.

"Remember, they all once lived ordinary human lives, just like you. Their paths and times in history may have been different, but they all achieved the transition from a fragmented state of being to a unified state of being.

"Many people know about the lives of the Unified Spirits I named, but you can also encounter a person at any station in life who could be one, even though the person's appearance gives you no hint of it. You can't tell from the outer trappings, only by the actions and totality of the life lived.

"That is why Unified Spirits are rarely recognized by contemporary society for what they truly are. It takes people looking back on the total life of a Unified Spirit for people to finally see who and what they were."

"So, are you saying that this unification of the Selves and the Baker—the subconscious—is what we're here to do? Is that the true purpose of life?"

"Yes, that's a major part of it. You are also here to assist other beings in the same quest. The task of living a human life could be conceived of as learning to understand your nature and directing it toward what you want. Even at the lower levels, your thoughts have the power to help you create what you want.

"But when you achieve awareness and control of the Lesser Self, letting the Greater Self guide you intuitively, and allowing the subconscious mind to do its job, you're truly free to create an existence of inner peace and harmony that will lead to becoming a Unified Spirit one day."

The Firemaker paused, then said, "Helen, don't be overly concerned with the details of what I've told you. The System can be reduced to four very simple statements:

"First, the Lesser Self is the *Desiring Self,* a kind of infant consciousness.

"Second, the *Facilitator* or subconscious mind — the one we're calling the Baker — is the active agent who brings together and mixes the ingredients of our desires.

"Third, the Greater Self is the *Knowing Self* that always tries to lift you above the Lesser Self.

"Fourth, once those three entities are in complete unison, the *Unified Self* is realized."

"Yes," I said, nodding. "I think I understand it now. At least most of it."

"Excellent. This is such a pivotal lesson and I know there's been a lot to absorb, but I want to push you just a little further. Do you think you can take a bit more on this subject?"

SEVEN DOORS OF THE FIREMAKER

CHAPTER 20

THE CAVE

"Yes, Firemaker, please go on. It's obvious that without this knowledge about how we evolve spiritually and psychologically, just passing through the doors won't get me where I need and want to be.

"I mean even after all I have learned in the Land Behind the Doors, look at what silly choices I made at the Bakery. Clearly I have a long way to go and I need this *right now*."

"Very well, that's some very good insight about your growth Helen. Don't be too hard on yourself, though. Notice that instead of judging all the other people at the Bakery, you are just being introspective about your own actions. That's an enormous change in your point of view and self-control from the first few doors.

"Now, I want to remind you that, while it helps to think of the Lesser Self, the Greater Self and the Facilitator or subconscious mind as three separate entities for clarity's sake, in fact *there is no separation*. All of Life is a continuum, and that is true of your existence.

"Now, I want you to think of a long, narrow cave that gets narrower and narrower at the back until the space is so small that a person standing up can touch both sides and the roof easily. Imagine that, from there, that person can see a tiny point of light far, far away at the opening. The cave slopes upward toward that light at the opening, making climbing all the way up and out extremely challenging.

"Next, think of the Lesser Self as existing at the narrow back of the cave down where there isn't much light and almost no space.

"Obviously, if we move up the cave toward the open end, the further we proceed, the more space and light there is. That forward, outward motion is the Self expanding.

"When it's way down at the bottom, there is little room to move, not much to light the way, and it is very easy to imagine that this is all there is or ever could be.

"But by constantly looking to the Light and moving toward it, the Self expands, sees more possibilities for growth, and, over time, reaches the opening of the cave where there are no walls, only space and light.

"However, during this process, everyone goes up, then slips back down, many, many times. You may not go all the way back to the bottom when you slip—what the people in the Auditorium would call 'bottoming out'—but you *will* slip, then rise, slip, then rise.

"Eventually, your rises will far outnumber your slips downward, and you will exit the cave once and for all.

"When that point is reached, a being has become a Unified Spirit and there are no further limits or lack of opportunity for that being. *Anything* is possible, everything lies open and before you at that place.

"Every single being is heading there eventually. It may not happen within the confines of the limited existence of one Earthly personality, but you are not your personality. When there is no longer a Helen Brower on Earth, there will still be a *you*, growing, expanding, and reaching into the Light forever. Do you see?"

By now I had tears in my eyes, the beauty of the concept was so overwhelming. "Oh yes, Firemaker, I see. And it's a great relief to know this. It means that slipping and going backward isn't the end of the world. And, even more important, that what we call 'death' is...well, not much really."

"Wonderful. I'm glad you understand. You are infinite. And you will get there.

"Helen, I know that this has been a lot to take in, so let's leave it for now. Because, if you're ready, I believe it's time for you to move on to the Sixth Door."

"Okay, but I have to confess, Firemaker, I still have so many questions left."

"Yes, and eventually they'll *all* be answered, but the next door awaits—unless you need a rest or don't wish to continue," she said gently.

"No, no, I'm ready. Here I go." She pointed to the door in front of me with a little blue sailboat painted on its tile and I moved toward it.

SEVEN DOORS OF THE FIREMAKER

CHAPTER 21

THE SIXTH DOOR: THE SAILBOAT

As I stepped through the Sixth Door I realized that, unlike the other doors so far, I recognized this place. This was the inlet on the Little Dreamy I had seen that first day I met Peri. The little blue sailboat was still tethered to the dock, the water gently lapping against her sides.

She was so sweet and perfectly sized for me that I had to peek inside. On the bottom of the hull, stacked neatly on top of a metal case not much larger than a hatbox, was a small piece of paper folded like a fan and a brass compass the size of my fist.

I couldn't resist getting a closer look, so I boarded her, picked up the paper, and unfolded it. It was a map charting the location of a group of islands in a delta not far from the inlet. Inside the metal case I found enough rations — a sandwich and thermos of water, crackers, dried fruit and nuts — for a day trip.

The map showed the Little Dreamy emptying out into a delta along with six other small rivers. On the other side of the delta, where the fresh water joined with the sea, there was a group of islands that didn't seem far from where I was sitting in the little boat. If that was where I was going, I hoped that meant this would be a quick trip.

After studying the map a little, I spotted a small green arrow and suddenly felt compelled to go to where it pointed. Unfortunately, back then, not only was I no sailor, I'd never even *been* sailing. What's more, when it comes to directions, I don't know east from up. And, just as important, water and I never had a complete reconciliation after the time I got lost in the heart of the undertow when I was a little girl.

I was about seven, I think, and the family was spending a rare week of vacation at the beach. I wasn't familiar with swimming in the ocean at all, and I managed to find the riptide right off the bat.

Fortunately, before I ran out of kicking and flapping power, a lifeguard appeared. He knew how to take me parallel to the shore rather than swimming head on against the riptide, and that saved me. For that ninety-second eternity before he got to me though, when I couldn't breathe or even see the shoreline, the seven-year-old me was sure that I wouldn't make it out of there.

I didn't *completely* quit the water after that. I still swam a little if I thought it wasn't too deep, but I never went into it again with the same fearless confidence I'd had before.

That meant that meeting the challenge of the Sixth Door, sailing out all by myself, was going to take a real leap of faith.

I looked at the map, then at the compass, then at the map again. These should have been enough, but since I had no idea how to sail, I was at a loss and about to get out of the boat and look for help when I saw a small bundle of rope coiled near the tiller with a note pinned on the top.

"Pull Me," it read, which I did, instantly setting off a series of events: the boom slid over my head and the sail fluttered loudly; then it filled with a gust of wind as the little boat leaned over and began to move away from the shore.

At first I was shaky about being on the water all alone, but I finally managed to relax a little, then, when things went well, a little more, and then, when nothing bad happened, a whole lot more. I sailed easily for an hour or two. The boat seemed to know what it was doing, and that was a good thing, since *I* certainly didn't.

Then, unexpectedly, the breeze that had so softly carried me this far quickened, and I soon found myself battling angry winds and fierce currents. I was in big trouble.

Blinking back the tears, my heart pounding, I bore down on the rudder trying to keep the boat on course, but she had a mind of her own and sailed into the storm, riding high atop the waves, and then plummeting suddenly into the troughs.

The boat struggled desperately to climb a wall of water that had replaced the once safe sky, and we were pitched again atop the waves, bow pointed toward the heavens.

This went on and on for what seemed like hours. Frantically trying not to be thrown overboard or have my head cracked open by the boom, I tied myself to the boat with a rope and began bailing water as fast as it poured in.

I managed to save myself from those fates, but my efforts to take control of the situation were useless. All I gained was a pair of blistered hands and a face pounded numb by the driving rain. I was in the fight of my life, terrified as the wind and the seething river spat the little boat back and forth at their mercy.

Until now in the Land Behind the Doors, when I was afraid or couldn't imagine a way out, I'd cry out for The Firemaker. But this time was different. While my Lesser Self wailed inside, my Greater Self stayed in charge and I chose instead to stick it out on my own, fueled by a surge of inner resolve that gave me the strength to carry on through those awful hours.

After a seemingly endless night of struggle, morning finally came and, with it, the end of the storm. It was a great relief — for about as long as it took me to catch my breath.

Soon, however, I realized that my troubles were *not* over. I was past the delta and out to sea. Land was just a faint outline on the horizon, and now I was adrift with no wind or current to take me back to shore.

Where only a short time ago there'd been too much wind, now there was too little. No breeze, no movement, no end in sight. It was as if a drought had come and turned my world into a place of stillness and silence so impenetrable that I could do little more than *be*. The day was hot and my windbreaker was my only shelter against the sun.

The bit of shade was critical to my survival, but it didn't help maintain the resolve that had gotten me through the storm. It was slipping away, and with the lowering of the sun I felt a similar lowering of my Self.

The thought of another night adrift was almost unbearable. Only flashes of courage from my Greater Self kept me from losing hope completely, but there were moments when I had almost none, when my thoughts were as bleak and dark as the night that closed in around me.

All that night I was restless and full of doubt. Why had I done this to myself? Why had I put myself in harm's way? I could be safe now, on dry land, all curled up in the green hammock in The Garden.

But even as I lamented my predicament, inside I knew that my decision to follow The Firemaker had not been wrong. Had I not chosen to go on this journey, my chronic restlessness, which was never far away, would have taken hold again, driving me from the sanctuary I had found in Peri's garden.

Finally the sun reappeared and though I waited all that day, there was still no wind. Feeling lost and alone, I cautiously rationed my food and the last drops of water from my thermos.

Then, at last, just as the sun went down again, the breeze freshened a little and softly filled the sails, gently washing the boat toward a small island.

Just off shore where the water was shallow enough, I put on my windbreaker, gathered the map, compass, and what was left of the provisions, hopped out and carefully dragged the boat high onto the beach, grateful to be on dry land again.

Now the moon had risen, and the evening was swiftly growing cool. In my damp clothes, I was beginning to tremble from the cold.

I made my way up a small rise to a grove of trees growing near the water's edge and found shelter under their dark branches. I was exhausted, hungry and thirsty, but the sound of the night breeze rustling through the leaves soothed me, and I promptly fell into a deep sleep.

CHAPTER 22

THE PAINFUL WHITE ORB

I don't know what time it was when I awoke, maybe three o'clock in the morning. But in spite of my weariness and half-closed eyes, I immediately saw something shimmering in the dark not more than five yards away.

I got up, walked over, reached down slowly and cautiously touched it. The size and shape of a soccer ball, it was opalescent and warm to the touch. Something compelled me to pick it up, just as something had compelled me to follow the green arrow.

Its heaviness was unexpected, as was the wave of pain that instantly surged through my body when I touched it, causing me to lose my balance.

Stumbling backwards, I flung it away, not with the intention of destroying it, but to be rid of the pain. It fell hard against a bolder and shattered into a heap of gritty white powder.

Unsure if I'd done a good or a bad thing, I dropped to my knees and saw something that made my eyes fill with tears. Lying amidst the rubble was a small stone, bright and beautiful beyond belief. I knew instantly what it was.

Scooping it up and placing it over my heart, there came the feeling of seeing your best and dearest friend after years and years of separation. It was complete, whole, fulfilling.

As the stone rested there, something miraculous began to happen. It was as if a vault in my mind, long locked and sealed, was swinging open. Light came flooding in and the forgotten memory of a little girl searching for a piece of the sun poured into my consciousness. The feeling was pure joy, and I knew it was true.

It *was* true! I had finally found my Sunstone!

But just then, the wind began swirling and darting, reminding me how cold I was and that there were still hours to go before morning. The Sunstone in hand, I began searching for tinder and kindling to make a fire. By its light, I soon found dry twigs and branches downed by the storm.

I didn't have any matches, but my intuition told me that, by striking the edge of the Sunstone against something solid like a sharp rock, it would make sparks and yet not be damaged.

At first the twigs wouldn't catch, but I remembered the Supreme Law. I *believed* I could do this and took action to support that belief. I kept at it, and on the seventh or eighth try, I got a small fire going.

I was very pleased with myself, I must say, and suddenly everything was just so, well, *clear*.

It was as if I'd never seen fire before. Looking back, it seems elementary now. But in a way that was true—I had never really *seen* fire before, at least not like I was seeing it right then.

I thought back to that first day on the bus with Virgie and that voice in my head asking, "What *other* miracles are you ignoring in your life, Helen?"

I marveled at how the darkness receded as the flames grew. With each new log, the night shrank, and I could see ever more vividly where I was.

It seems almost silly when I say this because it's so obvious, but as I said, I had never paid attention to fire before. It brings light and moves back the darkness, but I'd always taken all the elements of fire as one lumped-together event, and not really appreciated what actually happens step by step.

The fire continued to grow, and the bigger it got, the smaller my fears became. Then, suddenly, that old, familiar cold place in the center of my chest squeezed tight one last time, then burst into nothingness, destroyed by the heat of the fire and my determination to complete my journey through the doors.

I'd had to go through six of the Seven Doors and also face my fear of water to achieve this feeling, but now so many things were visible that I hadn't seen before. Everything was as clear to me as the bright red, orange and yellow flames dancing in front of my eyes.

Until this moment I'd been tired and sad, with a heart full of nearly abandoned dreams. I'd forgotten who I was, deep down in the center of me. My truth had become buried under layer upon layer upon layer of ill-formed beliefs about who I was and who

I was not. They'd always been half-truths and really were nothing more than self-perpetuated lies.

The realization was overwhelming to me. I felt the way an animal must feel when it's been caught in a snare but somehow manages to free itself. I threw back my head into the night, flung my arms toward the stars and cried out, "I've smashed the Pearl! NO MORE DARKNESS!"

The feeling of relief was enormous, so complete and new that at first I didn't notice the return of the orange sky. Without my realizing it, the night had ended.

My gaze fell on the map, and I was surprised to see something I hadn't been aware of until now. I picked it up and looked at it more closely.

In addition to the large green arrow, there was another symbol—a little yellow star marking Star Island downstream from the direction I'd fought to go. Instinctively, I knew this was where I was now.

At that moment, a breathtaking insight came to me. Struggling to go where I thought I *should* go, I'd fought against the elements as I'd always fought against everything that was easy and good and right for me.

All my life I'd insisted on sailing *upstream*! All my life I'd been unaware that I could never, ever find the happiness I sought anywhere but on the current that ran naturally in the other direction—the direction of my Downstream Dream of Wholeness.

I wanted to know more of this island, so I began to walk inland. A gentle wind blew off the river and calmed whatever restlessness remained in my heart. The deep silence gave me steadiness, and the open space and sweet scents provided my soul with still-ness.

Just when I was desperately thirsty, I came across a little freshwater stream, a gift from The Firemaker I'm sure. I drank my fill, topped off my thermos and ate the last half of the stale sandwich from my rations. It was hard and chewy, but I was so hungry that it tasted like ambrosia.

My newfound peace of mind filled me with a delicate solace that enabled me to walk for hours at a time without fatigue or discomfort. This island of harmony was a place I instinctively knew was as much a part of me as the color of my eyes and the shape of my hands.

I was expanding quickly inside, becoming more aware of my truest desires, needs and wants, and seeing that they resided in my Downstream Dream and nowhere else. To find them, I had to go in the direction of the flow, sometimes riding it out if it got rough, but relaxing and trusting rather than pushing against it.

The Downstream Dream lived inside me, had always been there, always available for me to care for and nurture into my life. It was embedded in every fiber and cell of my being, in everything I loved. Soft and accommodating, it whispered to me like the distant tone of a bell, a sound that lingered but did not deafen by insisting on overriding my Free Will.

Surely I could have reached some mediocre up-stream destination. With perseverance, I probably could have made it to some version of the City of Stability and been afraid to leave it, calling it good enough. I'd spent my whole life up to that point doing some version of exactly that. Lots of people do.

But now I knew that, even if I'd achieved that objective, I would never have been at peace. Only by following my Downstream Dream could I find what I truly needed, and that could all be revealed to me through the guidance of my heart.

Now I knew better than to be suspicious of what came to me on gentle currents. Now I knew better than to think that if something came easily, it had no value.

It was true, *belief plus action is the Supreme Law of Life* because if you believe you can't do something, it's crystal clear that you can't.

But if you believe you *can*, and you *do something* to accompany that belief, just about everything is possible.

I thought of Thomas Edison and the thousands of tries he made before finding the correct material for the light bulb filament. He believed he could do it, and he did it. That kind of belief is the same thing that got people to the top of Mt. Everest the first time and to the moon and back.

Yes, *belief plus action is the Supreme Law of Life*, I understood that now. And there was something else, too.

My whole life I'd been waiting for something outside me to fill my inner emptiness. Now, I knew everything I could ever want or need was inside me, inside the Downstream Dream of Wholeness that is the very core of who I am.

Though I had nearly lost the ability to see or hear or feel it, it lived on beneath the hurt, regret and disappointment that covered its brightness, *my* brightness!

The Sunstone was mine, had been with me all the time, but shrouded inside the Pearl. To find it, I had to go through that darkest of dark nights.

I had to look at myself straight on and claim, finally and passionately, to know that I was done with the past. From now on, to chart my course, I would look to the future and downstream to find my way.

SEVEN DOORS OF THE FIREMAKER

CHAPTER 23

BETTER EYES

As I explored the island, I knew that eventually The Firemaker or the next door would appear. Sure enough, just when I felt I'd been there long enough, I turned a corner in a small valley and came on a signpost shaped like a pointing hand. It read:

THIS WAY TO THE GARDEN

A few yards more, and I saw The Firemaker waiting for me. I was thrilled to see her.

"Hello, Helen," she said.

"Firemaker! Hello! I'm soooo glad to see you again! The island was just incredible. This whole journey is incredible!"

"So, you've gotten around to enjoying yourself?" The Firemaker said.

"So much has happened! And, to answer your question, yes! I *have* been enjoying myself. All of this adventure, the discoveries, victories and insights about life in general — it's amazing. I'm still taking it all in of course, but everything is making more and more sense and starting to come together."

"And how do you feel physically?"

"A little shaky, to be honest. That was a pretty rough ordeal. But I'm calm on the inside and, while I know it's hard to believe, I'm happy."

"Any other thoughts?"

"Well, to tell the truth, I still don't like a lot of the negative things that humans do in the world. Like the desecration of the natural world and all this insane violence against each other, both physically and psychologically. Not to mention the greed and dishonesty and all of that.

"But now I understand that dissatisfaction with it is also what drives me to want to grow and make sure that *I'm* not contributing to that.

"And if I grow enough, I'll help change those things while I'm here. That feels pretty darned good.

"I've also realized that drawing quick conclusions based on the outcome of an individual or a collective act can be a mistake.

"This is like having better eyes. It's that simple."

The Firemaker nodded. "Go on."

"Okay. Well, I've learned so much about Free Will and how powerful it is in our lives, and about how, whether we realize it or not, we generate what we receive. I've learned that it's extremely easy to rant and rave about how bad things are, but what I need to concentrate on is how *I participate* in creating my own reality.

"So if I'm creating it, why don't I just stop bitching about it and change what I'm creating? That makes a whole lot more sense."

I paused for a moment, and then added, "I've also learned it's not that *easy* to give full attention to all that's actually going on."

"Yes, that's a large part of it. Anything else?"

"Well, I feel so much better than I have for a long time. I feel like I did as a little girl. You know, in love with life.

"Somewhere along the way I'd forgotten about joy. I just got lost in the Mists of Circumstance, struggling against life rather than letting myself go with it to my Downstream Dream of Wholeness where I truly wanted and needed to be."

"And now?"

"Now I know the difference. And I know that I was living almost exclusively in my Lesser Self.

"So it's obvious that my choices were, by default, Lesser Self choices. I mean, what else could they have been, given the results? Simply knowing that one truth changes everything.

"It's challenging but also incredibly comforting. I don't feel utterly confused at the core. And you know what else? I'm starting to notice how beautiful things are. Little things that I used to take for granted, like a single pebble, or the true nature of fire. I realize now that I'd totally forgotten how to *see!*"

"You're blossoming, Helen. Growing from the seed of your Lesser Self into the beautiful flower of your Greater Self."

"Thank you, Firemaker. I really am, aren't I?" I said, grinning broadly. "I'm starting to appreciate what that means."

The Firemaker nodded her head.

"You know, I almost called for you when I was in that little blue boat during the storm, but somewhere deep down inside I knew I'd be all right.

"Before traversing this latest door, I never thought so. Not really. Not like I do now. Clearly, I needed to discover all these things for myself."

"Yes, Helen. You weathered the storm, as I knew you would, and you found the sweetness and joy of your Downstream Dream. As you claim it, you'll find aspects of your being that are waiting to be realized, and you'll begin to feel the wholeness and the self-unification you've longed for."

"That sounds religious or spiritual."

"Only if you want it to be. Your Free Will determines what it means to you. For someone with a religious or spiritual inclination, it becomes part of their nature. For someone who's not so inclined, or who's skeptical of such things, it's simply a scientific way of living. It works either way. I think you understand what I mean."

"Yes, I do. Even though I've absolutely, one hundred percent stumbled through it, everything seems so clear now.

"I've learned that not resisting isn't at all the same thing as surrendering. I didn't know that before.

"Surrendering is what you do when you're worn down, like I was during the storm. I *had* to surrender. I had no choice. It was a passive thing.

"But *not resisting* is an active choice. While I was waiting for the wind to bring me back to shore, I had to choose how I'd handle the waiting, the nothingness.

"I chose to still myself, to stay centered emotionally and to allow things to happen around me and for me. It must have been a little like that for Virgie and Peri when their husbands died."

"Yes, Helen," she said, "more and more you're realizing what you're capable of without outside help. Now you know that each door has been another level of learning attained and that each experience has removed another layer of falseness from you."

"True, Firemaker, but I can hardly believe, even after all that's happened, that it's really happened to me."

The Firemaker laughed softly. "Yes, I know these experiences have been out of the ordinary, but in order for you to learn to adapt to changing circumstances rapidly and without undue trauma, they've been absolutely necessary."

"Absolutely. *All* of this has been exactly what I needed. Now I feel I can go freely toward the things that nourish who I am."

"That's wonderful, Helen. Do you have any other thoughts before moving on?"

"Well, one thing continues to bother me. Despite my newfound confidence, I know I'll still have doubts. I imagine that I'm still going to be confused and afraid sometimes, especially when it comes to making decisions.

"That's never been easy for me, you know? When I have decisions to make and several of the choices are appealing, it just makes it worse. I get frazzled and crazy going round and round trying to figure out what to do.

"It makes me feel like one of those hamsters, you know the ones on a treadmill scurrying to nowhere as fast as their little legs can take them."

"Some of that's just life, Helen. There's always a little doubt. Even the truly great souls experience it.

But now when you feel confused, you can remember the lesson, the door that corresponds to the experience you're having.

"It will be helpful for you to hold this journey in your consciousness as a constant companion and a reference point to help you through the rest of your life."

I thought for a moment. "Yes, knowing that I can recall the lessons, revisit the doors so to speak, is reassuring. I like that. Sometimes life is messy and unclear, and deep down I know that's okay, but in the past I haven't been able to handle it very well.

"I guess, the truth is, Free Will still makes me a little nervous because I feel like one of those new drivers, those rookie *soul drivers* you talked about before who bang into each other.

"And now that I know just how much power we have through Free Will, it seems like a tremendous responsibility."

"There's a reason you feel this way, Helen. Your Lesser Self still believes you'll choose poorly, make a mistake, be judged and have to pay for your error.

"Let me explain..."

CHAPTER 24

THE RING

"You might consider this way of looking at it: unless there are immediate consequences to your actions, there's almost no way you can know for certain if you've chosen well or chosen poorly until later."

I must have looked perplexed because The Firemaker nodded and continued.

"Expecting that you'll be judged harshly for what you've chosen is a big part of a stubborn belief system that was ingrained in you from the time you were very young. Those experiences, among others, formed the core elements of the Pearl.

"As a child, negative outcomes were the only way you knew for certain if you'd acted appropriately or not. Punishment was your compass. It was one of the few reliable, if unpleasant, ways for you to know how you were doing at any given moment.

"But you have a much better compass now that you know the City of Joy is the place inside you that holds your Downstream Dream. Your Downstream

Dream is and will always be the most immediate and true compass you'll ever have.

"When you make any decision that moves you closer to your Downstream Dream, you'll feel a sense of relief, rightness and calm. If, however, your actions take you upstream, and there may be times you'll have to go there briefly, you'll feel tense, tired and disconnected from what really makes life worth living.

"Remember the white powder that was left on the ground after you smashed the Pearl on Star Island?"

"Yes, I do."

"Good, because it is an important symbol. You see, even though you've smashed the Pearl, and most of your pain and confusion has already dissipated, there will still be some residue surfacing for a while, maybe a long while. This is true for everyone who smashes the Pearl and that's what you're experiencing right now when you doubt yourself.

"A good example of this is that of a soldier who has been wounded with shrapnel from the explosion of an artillery shell. The shrapnel from that blast has been deeply embedded in the soldier's tissues and will continue to work its way out of the body and to the surface for many years.

"True, the soldier has lived through the initial explosion of the armament, or in this case, the Pearl, and the major source of damage has been destroyed, but that doesn't eliminate *all* the smaller pockets of shrapnel that have been blasted deep into the physical or psychic body. Healing from that kind of damage doesn't happen all at once. It can take a long time for all those experiences and feelings to come to the surface and be dealt with once and for all.

"Be patient with yourself when you're feeling as if you should be further down the road in terms of your progress, Helen.

"Yes, you have accomplished much, seen much and learned much. But the residue from smashing the Pearl will still surface from time to time.

"When that happens, just remember that it's simply shrapnel surfacing, and that it's perfectly in line with the process required for growing beyond your past.

"But, I know you're still concerned about your ability to make good choices, so I'll give you a technique to help you focus when you feel confused."

The Firemaker pointed to the bag hanging around my neck. "Open your pouch," she said. Amazingly, the leather was as supple as it had been before the storm. I reached inside and found the coin.

"Toss the coin in the air, Helen. Toss it high."

Summoning the same intensity I'd used to spin the Big Deal Wheel, I pitched the coin high into the air. The moment I did, it began to change, its center opening and expanding to form a ring.

"Look up. What do you see inside the ring?"

The ring, at first small enough to fit on my finger, grew larger and larger as it ascended. Inside it I saw all the problems and difficulties I didn't know how to resolve. As I concentrated, the ring reached the apex of its arch and started back down.

"Quickly, Helen. Focus on one situation," The Firemaker said, "and tell me what it is."

"*Career,* Firemaker I've never really had one."

"Good choice. Now, untangle it from all the other situations that are clamoring for your attention and look into the center of the ring. Look with your heart for the truth. When you find it, you'll know what to do."

I focused on the ring with all my might. So strong was my intention to see, so powerful my will to act, the ring stopped falling abruptly, several feet above my head. It stayed there, hovering in the air, just slightly beyond my reach.

"What do you see?"

"I see the situation as it is by itself now, without a bunch of other stuff clouding it. I know and feel things about it I couldn't before.

"Oh, my gosh, Firemaker! I know what I am supposed to do!"

"Excellent. But don't tell me. Just put it in your heart for later.

"Now take the ring."

I had to stretch onto the very tips of my toes to reach it. In the last moment before I took hold of it, I lost my balance. The ring began to fall and I had to lunge to grab it.

"Good catch, Helen. What do you see now?"

"I see just exactly what's been blocking me deep down, beneath all the static about what I should do and how I should feel."

Then the ring flattened out and became a coin again, but by now too much had happened for me to marvel at the transformation. I slipped it back into the pouch as I gathered my thoughts.

"Do you know what you'll do now?"

"Yes, Firemaker, I do. In choosing my career, or rather the lack thereof, to focus on, and by putting the ring around it, I had to let go of all the other problems for the moment. In that moment I saw the truth and knew what I wanted.

"I also saw that my habit of gathering problems together and worrying over them all at the same time only exhausts and confuses me.

"The little details and upsets I have about each situation get all tangled up and I can't see my way through. But I've got it now. I need to look at each situation by itself and draw a little ring around it in the center of my heart."

"Yes, that's right. Anything else?"

"I must consider which Self is involved in the seeing."

"Very good, Helen. That's excellent."

"It's always my Lesser Self that's confused, isn't it?"

The Firemaker nodded.

"It's that Baby Self. It just doesn't want to give up wanting things to be a certain way. When I chose the problem I focused on, I suddenly realized I'd been hoping for an outcome different than the one I really needed.

"I wasn't letting my Greater Self guide me or the Baker prepare and deliver the loaf. I was keeping myself from the truth, and that was preventing me from knowing what to do."

"The Firemaker nodded again and then turned, pointing toward the west.

"You've done extremely well through the first six doors. I think you're ready to finish the journey now, Helen. Am I right about that?"

I smiled and didn't hesitate. "Yes, Firemaker. I most certainly am."

SEVEN DOORS OF THE FIREMAKER

CHAPTER 25

THE CHOICE

I might have thought I was ready to finish my journey, but The Firemaker was about to throw me a curve ball. She pointed to a little path and said, "That way to the last door. Go ahead. I'll follow."

We walked up the winding path for a minute or two, turned a corner, and came to a fork in the path. A few feet up each of the two trails stood a door.

"Wait a minute!" I protested. "You told me there were only *seven* doors! I see *two* up there! That makes *eight*!"

"No, Helen, that's not correct. I said you needed to *pass through seven doors*. I never indicated that there weren't more than seven."

I shielded my eyes from the sun, scrutinizing each of the two doors. Neither had a tile, but when I concentrated, one door flashed an image of a candle in a cave, the other an image of a lotus flower in the center of a flame.

"So, I guess all that stuff about how to choose comes into play right here and now, huh?"

"Yes, Helen, It does," said The Firemaker, with a smile in her voice.

"Okay, I can do this," I said under my breath, and then a little louder:

Belief plus action is the Supreme Law of Life

Then I reached into the pouch and took out the coin, turning it to the face that read:

INSIDE

I tumbled the coin over and over in my fingers as I gave myself a pep talk. "Helen, this isn't about your whole life, all your problems, where you've been, or what you might have done better. It's just about picking the correct door *right now*."

With that I flipped the coin into the air and saw it expand once more into a ring. In an instant I saw the lotus in the flame and knew without a doubt which door I had to pick.

As the realization came to me, the ring returned to its original state as a coin and dropped neatly into my hand.

I smiled at The Firemaker and with no qualms walked up the path and stepped squarely in front of the door I'd chosen.

"I'm going in here," I said confidently.

Then I opened the Seventh Door.

CHAPTER 26

THE SEVENTH DOOR: THE POOL

I t's difficult to explain how sure I was that this was my door, but in some deep way I can't really name, I felt infinitely strong as I stepped through it. I knew I belonged there, and I expected to be bowled over by something utterly magical on the other side.

After all, this was my seventh and last door. Unfortunately, it wasn't all that magical.

Instead of the fabulous finale I'd imagined, I stepped knee-deep into an extremely nasty, foul-smelling swamp, stubbed my toe on something under the water and immediately fell face down in the muck.

"What the????" I shouted, covered from head to toe in black mud and some kind of creepy vines.

"Great! So much for my choosing abilities! I chose the Crap Door!!!"

Just then, a voice croaked: "Maybe not. Maybe not. Maybe not."

"What? Who? Who said that?" I heard a huge *kersplash*! Then, a frog the size of a football landed on a rotting log right next to my leg. "I said it! I said it! I said it!"

"Well, who the heck are you?" I demanded.

"Tour guide. Tour guide. Tour guide."

"Tour guide. What kind of dismal tour is this?"

"Tour of the past. Tour of the past. Tour of the past."

I shook my head and squeegeed as much mud off my face with both hands as I could. "Why am I not surprised?" Having been through so much before, I finally had to laugh at this mess.

By this time, I'd long since realized that the Land Behind the Doors could hold *anything*, and that sooner or later, so far anyway, it all ended up making sense.

"Okay, I'm game. Lemme have it."

"Walk to the end. Walk to the end. Walk to the end," the frog said.

I looked around. The place was thick with curly, snaking vines and floating debris of every description, but there seemed to be only one possible way that I could move, so I started in that direction.

"This way, I assume?"

The frog hunkered down, and I could see that he was about ready to spring.

"That's the way. That's the way. That's the way," he croaked. Then he lifted off for parts unknown and disappeared.

"Some tour guide," I muttered.

With no other obvious options, I slogged along for what felt like hours through the swamp. I soon found that it held everything I had ever worried about or feared would come to pass. These were the things I'd hoped to leave behind but dreaded would revisit me sooner or later because, essentially, I was all messed up and deserved it.

Clearly this was part of the residue, the shrapnel left over from smashing the Pearl that The Fire-maker had mentioned.

There were rusted tin cans and empty soda bottles, cracked teapots and old tires floating everywhere. Each object was labeled on the side with a word like *scarcity, fear, isolation, illness, addiction, despair, failure, dishonesty, greed, gossip, laziness.*

I was in the Swamp of the Past all right, knee deep in my former life, up to my armpits in Upstream struggles.

The further I went, the more I wanted to leave it all behind me forever and never look back. All I wanted was out.

After what seemed like forever in that hell, I finally heard the sound of rushing water. The thought of being out of the swamp and able to wash off the muck of the past gave me renewed energy and I pressed on.

Soon, I could see a little stream running off the edge of a cliff above, and a beautiful crystal waterfall about a hundred yards from where the swamp dried up and turned into a muddy bank.

With some real effort, I extricated myself from the swamp and mud, ran to the little waterfall and dove straight under it. The water was icy and invigorating, and, with abandon, I scrubbed myself clean of the Debris of the Past. I wanted it off me badly and washing it away felt so good that I couldn't help but giggle.

While I was bathing, I spied a lovely meadow no more than a half-mile away. When I was clean again, I headed directly for it. As I walked, a cool summer breeze moved across the landscape, caressing my skin and causing the grass to wave like lovely bolts of green satin for as far as I could see into the horizon.

On the way to the meadow, I realized that every door, including this one, had been both challenging and exhausting, but ultimately exhilarating, even if it took a while for the positive feelings to set in. Even though I hadn't chosen it, I had no end of curiosity about what was behind the *other* door, the one with the tile picturing the candle in the cave. Just a little peek would have been nice, you know?

Still, I knew I was in the right place, especially after having passed through the Swamp of the Past and the Purifying Waterfall. At last, I was completely done with all that darkness and pain.

It was lovely in the wide warmth of the sweet meadow, and the quiet afternoon sounds of insects and birds made me so relaxed and drowsy, I lay down to rest. Just at the edge of my awareness, like the gauzy end of a dream, a vision rolled onto the shores of my mind as I hovered between sleeping and waking.

It was completely different than the images I'd seen in the Auditorium. These images were full of wonder. I saw myself being and doing the things I held deep within the center of my heart— possibilities I'd previously thought of as nothing more than fantasies and daydreams. In this vision, I was surrounded by people who loved me and whom I loved deeply. I was strong, healthy, happy and fulfilled, like a beautiful sun-drenched flower opening to the warmth that embraced and surrounded it like the air of The Garden.

This was how my life could be, and it was available to me from the blueprint of my own dreams and the deepest desires of my own soul. All I had to do was choose.

When I opened my eyes, I saw something I hadn't noticed before. Just a few feet away, where the grass thinned, a gentle path led to an oval shaped pool filled with beautiful turquoise water.

I knew intuitively that it held my happiness, and I got up and walked toward it. When I reached the pool, I waded without hesitation into the shallow end, and then moved in further to where the water was chest-high.

I was so lost in my joy that I was surprised and a little bewildered to hear, "Does that feel good to you, Helen?"

"Wha…? Oh, yes, Firemaker! Almost unbearably good."

"This beautiful place is called the Pool of Possible Futures. It's built on your greatest truths and filled with all the wonderful futures you long for in your heart of hearts.

"The Swamp of the Past is its complete opposite. It's built on your most negative beliefs, the ones that only a short time ago you claimed daily through thoughts of fear, negation and lack.

"You're free to choose the reality in which you wish to swim. Regardless of appearances, regardless of how dire a situation seems—everyone is free to make that choice, although most never know it.

"As you make this choice, be sure to remember that what you think and what you feel, what you speak and do, have more impact on your life than you've ever imagined. Pay attention to these things for they issue from your beliefs and from your heart and they are the seeds of your tomorrows.

"You and you alone, Helen, have the power to create your future. Name what you want and claim it. Choose who you truly are and be it."

I thought for a moment. This was exhilarating stuff, but it was sobering too. If I understood The Firemaker correctly, we are all in a constant state of creating, and it begins with what we create inside ourselves.

Whether I viewed it scientifically, psychologically or extended it into the realm of religion and spirituality, the truth was still truth. I'd have to be in one place or the other, the Pool of Possible Futures or the Swamp of the Past. Which one I ended up in was up to me.

"Shall I go on?" The Firemaker asked.

I swam a little closer to her and said, "Yes, Firemaker, please do."

"Very well then. This knowledge you've just acquired is both practical and philosophical, and it works regardless of how one might perceive the mechanics. On a practical level, it's a framework for understanding the process of goal attainment.

"Suppose you're proceeding toward a goal—something arduous yet full of heart, like becoming a doctor, though it could be anything you felt called to achieve. By doing whatever the rules say you must do to finish, if you direct your will and don't falter, you will end up achieving your goal and becoming a doctor.

"On the philosophical level, understanding how goal attainment works begins with realizing what your Downstream Dream really looks like. In effect, you start at the end, believing you have the ability to be a wonderful doctor, ally and caregiver to your patients.

"Once you've fully seen that in your mind, you allow yourself to flow backwards through the stages of development that deliver up the goal, the medical degree, the years of training, and the physician's license.

"Call it what you want, psychological or spiritual, and put it in whatever terms are comfortable for you, but the two processes aren't really very different, no matter which way you approach the challenge of becoming a doctor."

"I understand, Firemaker," I said as I lowered my body deeper into the pool.

It was exquisite and I knew without a doubt that I had definitely chosen the correct Seventh Door.

SEVEN DOORS OF THE FIREMAKER

CHAPTER 27

TRACKS

Deep in thought, I floated in the pool, recalling everything that had happened, all the learning and the new understandings that came with each door. I felt as if I could stay in the pool forever, just existing. But I also knew that, as sweet and glorious as it was, there was more, much more, to do. There was a whole new life to be lived.

A little flutter in my heart told me there was something more for me to see, and I knew it was terribly important.

By now I'd come to accept what that meant. As amazing as new vision is, it rarely seems to come without a good bit of roll-up-your-sleeves hard work.

"There will always be more to learn, Helen," The Firemaker said. "Perhaps what you're feeling is the need to gather your experiences together from the perspective of where you are now while they're still so new. This may be a good time for you to revisit the doors."

"Yes," I said. "That sounds right."

CHAPTER 28

SEVEN DOORS OF THE FIREMAKER

The Firemaker asked, "Where would you like to begin, Helen?"

"Well, I guess it makes sense just to go in order from first to last."

"Very well," she said, nodding. "Let's look to the First Door, then.

"While you were in the amusement park, most of the people you noticed, those spinning for personal gain, were there because of something called *Generalized Longing*.

"Like most human beings, they were looking for something to take the ache of that longing away.

"Unfortunately, unless a person has awakened to the Greater Self, the Big Deal Wheel often brings only more entanglement and less freedom, and the prizes it generates obscure, rather than fulfill, the core truths of the heart.

"To be really finished with the need to revisit such a place, one must know what it is she truly wants. But this can be very difficult. Often what one thinks she needs doesn't turn out to be what she thought it was or where she thought she would find it.

"Many of the people at the Wheel had no idea about their Downstream Dream. Without knowing one's true destination, it's not possible to ever be truly happy, at peace and fulfilled in life."

Her words, though not wholly unfamiliar, had an energizing effect, like an unexpected draught of cool air on a warm day. Hearing them now inspired me to a much larger vision. There was a reason my journey began at the Wheel amidst a throng of people.

I was beginning to understand that each of my lessons grew out of that one and joined to the next in a deeply purposeful way.

This wasn't just about *me*. It wasn't just about *my* journey. It was about *all* of us.

The entire picture was starting to come into focus.

She continued, "In order for you to eventually find your Downstream Dream, Helen, you had to stop spinning the Wheel so that you could move beyond the repetitive drama of Generalized Longing.

"Then, you had to confront the specific nature of your wound, the primal event or events where a part of you had become stuck. That's what the people behind the Second Door, in the Auditorium, were doing.

"It was in the Auditorium that you gained insight into your wound and the wounds of others. That's where you discovered the importance of letting the *wound identity* go when it becomes precious and forms the Pearl.

"You also saw how the Pearl had engulfed and obscured something you'd had inside all along, your piece of the sun. After that you came to realize the necessity of looking at others and yourself and at all of life through compassionate eyes.

"Behind the Third Door, you saw how the wound plays out in relationships. When you found the Beehive, you had the shocking experience of fully understanding that often those who have been hurt also sting viciously.

"Do you recall what the beekeeper told you just before leaving?"

"To wear a protective suit if I was going to go in or near the hive."

The Firemaker nodded. "Yes, a suit to protect you from being stung. But, as you know, that's no simple task. Dealing with bees can be a dangerous business.

"The more one is stung, the less resistant one becomes to the effect, though the desire for what bees offer doesn't seem to lessen. With enough stings, the body becomes allergic so that even a small amount of their poison can overwhelm the system.

"It was essential for you to really see what the Beehive represents and that being stung can not only hurt, but it can eventually make you very ill or even take your life away.

"Knowing that, and with the achievement of walking away without the sweetness of the hive, you saw that any relationship can contain sweetness or stings, and that some contain both.

"If you can't devise a suit for the ones with stings, you have to be smart enough and strong enough to walk away, no matter whom the relationship is with.

"With that awareness in place, it was easy for you to learn the lesson of the Fourth Door, Sugar and the Diner, and shift your perception to the idea that the standard of wholeness is in reality one, not two disguised as one.

"Relationships with other people are essential to healthy living, but only if the people involved are standing on an equal, visible, agreed-upon common base.

"Those experiences prepared you well for the Fifth Door, where you found the Bakery and learned about the complexity of your Subconscious Mind, your Lesser Self and Greater Self, and of the ultimate destination of integration into the Unified Self.

"With that knowledge, you entered the Sixth Door and boarded the little blue boat to face your biggest challenge, your lifelong fear of the water.

Alone, you found the strength to survive the battering storm, and the becalming of the boat, and ultimately found Star Island. That's where you smashed the Pearl and found your piece of the sun. It lifted your darkness and allowed you to see that the City of Joy exists inside *you*.

"That was your awakening, and it changed you forever. And, when it came time for the Seventh Door, you drew from within, symbolized by withdrawing the coin from the pouch and its transformation into a ring.

"Using that tool, you made a difficult choice and stepped forward, once again, into the unknown.

And, as it was with each door, you encountered a setback — or what *appeared* to be a setback.

"But, you pushed ahead, so much so that when you came to the Pool your choice was obvious and instantaneous. You chose to go ahead without reservation and pointed yourself in the direction of the Possible Futures waiting for you.

"You've done beautifully, Helen. With each door you passed through, you reclaimed another part of your wholeness. With each challenge you embraced, you activated another inner resource, one of the many inside you."

I felt like a bubble blown from a child's toy, a butterfly playing in a March breeze. I was so full of life and strength and joy I was about ready to burst.

SEVEN DOORS OF THE FIREMAKER

CHAPTER 29

THE TEACHERS BEHIND THE DOORS

"I know you're excited, but it may serve you to look again for a moment at the people you encountered along the way, what they were doing behind each door, and why they were there."

"Why they were there? Well, for so many of them, it was their pain, correct?"

The Firemaker nodded. "Yes. Many of the people at the Wheel spun because somewhere inside they knew their lives weren't whole. Others spun for noble purposes to relieve someone else's pain, and some spun to relieve their own.

"Some of the people in the Auditorium were ready to admit to themselves that something was terribly wrong with staying where they were, and others were content to stay in the City of Stability. But all had arrived there because of pain."

I thought for a moment. "And the women who were so desperate for sweetness to ease their pain that they kept going to the Beehive unprepared, pretending that the bees wouldn't hurt them."

"Yes, Helen, like those Sugar who waits on who look to the drug of romantic love to fill them and ease their hurt. In the end, all that running around only serves to distract them from their lives or, worse, sets them up to be dominated or abused by another partner or situation."

"As Sugar explained, that doesn't mean that one should be afraid of love or of entering into new settings and experiences; what it does mean is that one should go into it all with eyes wide open.

"Many experiences come to us in life. Some, on the less happy end of the continuum, are merely unpleasant, while others, the ones that seem hardest to let go of, are dangerous, or even life threatening, like one bee sting too many.

"A human being can only take so much injury before they become ill, in body or mind. It may occur little by little, or in one shattering moment from a tragically false step or poorly navigated decision driven by shame or inner pain, or perhaps by some other, unforeseen event.

"The experiences build upon each other, as you have seen, much like the gritty layers of a Pearl growing inside an oyster.

"When one repeatedly perceives that she is inadequate, a kind of deep inner confusion sets in. It can reach the point where she can even forget her True Nature and that she is the creator of the Pearl and not the Pearl itself.

"Regardless of what name one might give it, ultimately it's the sadness you've been carrying inside all these years, Helen, that's at the core of the Pearl. You have the eyes to see that now because you've worked to strip away the false ideas and beliefs crystallized at the deepest levels of your being.

"That's what you've done. You've smashed your Pearl and are nearly set free because of it. But there is one more piece you must have to complete the transformation from internal bondage to freedom.

SEVEN DOORS OF THE FIREMAKER

CHAPTER 30

THE SECRET

"Helen, if you can convert what I am about to say into awareness, there is nothing you cannot unlock, including relationships, your career, spirituality, all of it. It is the key that opens many of the Mysteries of Life."

The Firemaker motioned toward the back of the Pool, and, as I shifted my focus there, I saw the Seven Doors I had passed through. Now they were set side by side in an ancient, vine-covered stone wall. Each door had one word printed beneath the tile, forming a sentence. I read them out loud:

ALL...ILLNESS...COMES...
FROM...A...BROKEN...
HEART

And there it was. Seven little words, instantly clearing up so many things that had haunted my life.

With an elegant, simple stroke The Firemaker had shown me *why* I had to make it through seven doors, not five or even six. It *must be seven* or the Secret of the Broken Heart would be incomplete.

She was showing me the story of my life and handing me the key to everything that had dogged me, everything that I'd never understood about myself, or my parents, or my lovers or anyone else.

With it now so very clear, I could actually see the pathway of lived-through pain that connected the outer to the inner and the past to the present. I would never again be able to deny or ignore that I knew this.

I would never be able to pretend, as I had done before I began my journey, that walking around with a broken heart had nothing to do with how I felt or the choices I made. It had *everything* to do with it. Nor could I deny that *everybody* who intentionally inflicts pain on this planet is suffering from an illness and has a broken heart too.

"Remember the Secret of the Broken Heart and mark it well. Then you will bring great healing into the world. *All illness comes from a broken heart.* That includes the madness of murder, war, and all the other mayhem on Earth you asked about before.

"Doing harm is an illness, and it comes from a broken heart. And on Earth at this time, it is a pandemic, an invisible illness that afflicts virtually everyone, *either as a victim or perpetrator*, and it has been this way for thousands of years."

At last I understood what had been wrong with me, as The Firemaker had said, all those years, those long, lonely years. It was a moment of great relief, as my intense sadness lifted and dissipated like fog in the warm sun. But something was still nagging at me.

"Okay, I understand that when it applies directly, but what about when babies are born with physical or mental limitations? Obviously, they didn't experience a broken heart and end up in that condition."

"No, of course not. And the answer to that is in two parts: first, the Secret doesn't say that the broken heart that causes the illness has to be *yours*. In cases of genetic conditions, the broken heart may well have been that of the great-great-great-great grandmother or grandfather of the child. But the point at which the genetic changes took place that introduced the illness into the family line, it came from a broken heart.

"Second, a parent or parents can attract illness to the child out of worry, dread and a hyperactive imagination that focuses on danger to the baby. Parents can draw these things to their children, and the parents' fears that result in the child's illness *always* come from a broken heart."

"So you're saying that sometimes children are just stuck with something from birth and nothing can change that?"

"Certainly for many children the destruction caused by a broken heart, or a chain of broken hearts in one's genealogy, can have such impact that it's almost impossible to overcome. It shapes the child's environment to such an extent that his or her biggest challenge will be to cope with it. But in spite of that, great accomplishments have come from people who were burdened by tremendous physical challenges.

"Some well-known examples are Edison's and Beethoven's deafness. I'm sure that you can think of dozens more."

"Yes, I can see that very clearly now. I've always wondered about it because it seems so unjust. But as you've told me, I don't have all the information to understand everything fully, so I need to reserve my judgment.

"I will tell you, though, I'd have *never* thought of those things as explanations for why children suffer like the rest of us."

"As we've discussed, a lot of existence at this level has very rough edges from the human perspective, Helen. It can be very painful. Would you like to stop for a bit and reflect on all of this?"

I thought for a moment, then replied, "No, thank you. I'm okay. That fills in a lot of the blanks.

"Truthfully, I guess I thought I was done with all these questions, but now I understand about children who are ill, and I didn't before. And, as you said way back there after the Second Door with the Pearl and all, pain comes off the way it went on, in layers.

"Now that I know the Secret of the Broken Heart, it's plain to see how small I've been, and why I've lived such a mediocre existence when all along there were all the other incredible possibilities I could have chosen.

"Now I feel really clear. Going through the Seven Doors, and now this! It's like a miracle antidote against this malaise, this, this, *illness*. My broken heart is mending, Firemaker. I don't ever want to forget the Secret or the Lessons of the Doors. *Never*.

"You won't forget, Helen. You could choose to ignore all of this, but you will *never* forget it. This learning has become a part of you and will go forward with you as you create your future. That's what you've gained the ability to do, you see.

"You've earned the right to possess the Secret of the Broken Heart. That gives you the power to choose your most appropriate future and create it.

"The doors you've passed through and the Secret written on them are your guides. Remember their lessons and your heart will never be so easily broken again."

I sighed and nodded and felt a soft, inner calm rising in me. Yes, *the heart can heal the heart.* And my heart—if not completely unbreakable–was resilient, strong and incredibly alive. I was no longer lost in a fog and vulnerable. I had come home to the inside of me where my little piece of the sun had always lived. I was whole and free.

Even though her face was still hidden, I smiled at the woman in the cloak, a familiar and welcome sight.

SEVEN DOORS OF THE FIREMAKER

CHAPTER 31

THE FACE OF THE FIREMAKER

I felt empowered to ask what I'd wanted to ask all along. "Firemaker, will I ever be allowed to see your face?"

She laughed gently. "Certainly, Helen. Now that you have passed through seven doors, you can see my face anytime you like."

I swallowed hard. "Now?"

"Yes, now is the perfect time. Look into the surface of the water."

Looking into the pool that had become mirror still, I saw only my own reflection. There were no other images anywhere on the water, no clouds, no trees, nothing. Just me.

I looked up at The Firemaker and said, "I'm afraid I don't understand."

"Oh yes, Helen, you do. Somewhere *inside* you always have."

Now, very slowly The Firemaker pulled back her hood. I gasped as once again, I found myself looking at *my own face*.

But it was my own face transformed. There were no worry lines or shadows. My skin was full of life and color, and my eyes clear and bright as mountain spring water.

"I am the embodiment of your Unified Self, Helen. What you have seen in me is what you will eventually become by connecting *all that is in you to all that you are to be.*

"You've led yourself to yourself and now *you* are The Firemaker. Whenever you need to know what to do, remember the coin and the ring, and say these words:

I Am The Firemaker

I drew in a deep breath, completely overcome by what was taking place.

"Say the words now, Helen, and assume your True Place in life."

Innately I knew that what The Firemaker was saying was vital, yet it was so overwhelming and profound I could barely summon the courage.

But then, remembering all the doors I'd passed through, all the tests I'd undertaken and the Secret of the Broken Heart, I took in another deep breath, seized the moment and spoke the words aloud, albeit in a whisper: *"I am The Firemaker."*

As the last, hushed word fell from my lips the shimmering red gown dropped, empty, to the grass in a heap.

I stared in disbelief, hardly breathing. I swam slowly to the edge of the Pool, pulled myself up and cautiously stood where my guide and teacher through all this had stood. I called out to her, but she was gone. I was alone.

I stared at the gown, wanting to try it on but half expecting to be vaporized if I even touched it. That fleeting thought was immediately erased though, by my rapidly growing feeling of wellbeing.

At last I stepped into the gown and pulled it up around my shoulders. It fit flawlessly and felt wonderful against my bare skin. I shuddered with contentment.

As the gown settled around me, every muscle relaxed and I became aware of the little pouch that held the coin. I quickly opened it. It was a ring again, only this time exactly fitted to my finger. And on the outside, it bore the inscription:

I Am The Firemaker

Images of Virgie's hand and Peri's hand flashed through my mind and I instantly knew the ring belonged on the middle finger of my right hand, as they wore theirs. I slipped it on and then pulled the hood over my hair.

The moment I donned the hood, a beautiful white lotus emerged from the pond and burst into a magnificent flame of reds, yellows, blues and purples. The flame was bright, warm and alive—it didn't consume or scorch the lotus—and I knew that the fire was a living, eternal thing.

The flame was mesmerizing and enveloping, and then there was the feeling of being inside a giant kaleidoscope.

Everything was sparkling, moving, changing and *I* was changing. It was incredibly dizzying.

The Seven Doors, the people I'd met, the knowledge and insight I'd gained, all of it, flashed through my mind like lightning.

Then, suddenly, I was transported into the air and found myself floating above the scene of my bicycle accident. I was in it and yet not in it, an observer with no needs or wants, contented in a way I had never felt before. Centered.

I saw myself lying by the roadside, dressed in my gardening clothes. My bicycle was on its side just a few inches away from my head.

From my position above all of it I was wonderfully lucid. I knew who and where I was. And I knew that this was reality, but that what I'd just experienced at the Pool was reality, too.

Then, I watched as a paramedic truck arrived and a man and woman hurried out of the truck and over to my body, checked my vital signs and looked me over.

They put a collar around my neck and gingerly loaded me onto a gurney and into the back of the truck. As they sped away, I floated above the vehicle as it raced through the streets and into the parking lot of a hospital emergency room.

Now I felt myself falling toward my body and lost consciousness again. I don't know how much time elapsed, but when I woke up, I was on a bed in the emergency room. I was groggy and aching, but I knew instantly that I was not seriously hurt. The emergency medical technicians from the truck were still there, along with a doctor and two nurses.

The doctor flashed her small light into my eyes and said, "Welcome back, Helen. We just need to take a look at some X-rays to make sure, but so far it doesn't look like there's anything wrong with you that a day or two of rest won't cure."

The hospital staff busied themselves with whatever it was they were doing to me, checking for broken bones or other injuries, I guess. A nurse handed the doctor some X-rays and she walked into another room to have a look.

Just then, the young guy from the EMT team spoke, "You doin' okay, Helen?"

I smiled, "Yeah—I'm okay I think. Kinda woozy. My head hurts like crazy."

He nodded. "I would imagine. That was a heck of a thump you took against that curb. But you look pretty good, goose egg and all."

"And the little girl with the soccer ball? Is she okay?"

"Absolutely. You missed her by a mile. She's just fine."

"Thank goodness for that."

"Well, we'd better get out of doc's way and back on the road. Oh, this is Carrie and I'm Eric. Sorry about the circumstances, but it was still nice to meet you. You take care now."

I nodded back. "Yes, I will. Nice meeting you guys, too. Thank you both so much for helping me."

"Nothing to it. It's what we do. See you around, Helen." Carrie said with a little wave.

Eric waved too. "Bye for now," he said.

For now, I thought. Hmmm. I smiled back. "Okay, see you around."

Just then, Eric stopped, came back over and handed me my backpack. "Oh, I almost walked off with your stuff. By the way, we found Persephone's name and address on a check in your wallet. We gave her a call and she should be here soon. Hope that's okay. We couldn't find any other contacts for you."

"Oh yeah, thanks. That's great. She's my boss and best friend. Thank you Eric."

"No problem, Helen. See you."

I watched him walk away. And, while I don't know what it was exactly, maybe it was the way he said my name, I was sure we had things to do together.

I knew if that proved to be true, my journey behind the Doors had equipped me to handle it like a grown up. There would be no more Protos for me. I'd left *that* room a long time ago and was in a new one, a much better one, I was sure of it.

As Eric and Carrie stepped out of the sliding glass doors I impulsively reached for the pouch around my neck. Gone. A touch of disappointment stabbed me, but I caught myself and refused to drop into that scared, childish place, my Lesser Self.

I remembered exactly what to do and whispered, "I am The Firemaker."

The words brought a perfect sense of completion, strength and integration with my new conscious-ness. In the deepest center of my being, where the Greater Self resides, I knew the wisdom I'd been shown was the sure remedy to any petty fear my Lesser Self might conjure up.

I was The Firemaker now, and I knew I always would be. It was unnecessary, no, impossible, to go back to my old life, and I knew it. It felt wonderful!

I was whole and lit up from within by a piece of the sun as bright as the one I'd searched for so many years ago as a child.

Then I looked up and realized that Peri was there, standing over me, studying my face, concerned but smiling. I smiled, too, and held out my left hand to her.

The emergency room lights were very bright behind her and I shielded my eyes with my right hand, glimpsing the gold ring on my middle finger engraved with the words:

I Am The Firemaker

"Good Lord, honey. That was sure a nasty spill," Peri said. "Look at that goose egg on your noggin. Are you okay?"

I beamed and clutched her hand tighter. "Better than ever, Peri."

The doctor, who had walked into the other room briefly, came back. " Your X-rays look good, Helen. Nothing broken. Just a mild concussion. If you feel like it, we can let you go home as long as you don't drive."

"I'll drive her back over to my place," Peri said. "Nothing for her to do there but take it easy. I'll pamper her like one of my orchids."

The doctor nodded. "Sounds good. Don't go to sleep for about three or four hours. Unless your headache worsens, there's nothing for you to do really. Just check back in with us next week. Take it

213

easy for a couple of days, Helen. You'll be as good as new."

I smiled. "Thank you, doctor. Thank you so much for everything."

I stood up and, even though my head hurt and I was a little wobbly, I felt healthy, safe and strong. Peri steadied me as we went through the hospital doors and got into the car.

Outside, the rainstorm had passed and the sun was breaking out from behind marshmallow puffy clouds. It seemed to me as though I had never, in my whole life, seen such a stunning, heavenly display.

Peri put her arm around me and her bright blue eyes twinkled as she said, "The EMTs told me they'd asked the man in the house by where you crashed to look after your bike. You want to swing by and put it in the trunk, or would that be too much for you right now?"

"I'd like that. That old bike is my buddy, so sure, let's go and get her."

Peri drove us over and a nice, elderly gentleman went into his garage and rolled out my bike.

"Looks like it's in pretty good shape," he said, loading the bike into the trunk.

"Haven't seen one of these old Huffy bikes since my kids were kids. But how are you doing, young lady? Are *you* all right?"

"Yes, thanks, I'm fine. It's nothing that a couple of days' rest won't cure. Thank you so much for looking after my bike. I really appreciate it."

"You bet. Not a problem. Hope you're feeling better soon," he said with a wave, and walked back into his house.

Peri started the car and we headed for her place just a few blocks away.

"If I'm not mistaken, that was one powerful ride you were on while you were unconscious." She said with a smile.

I looked into those keen eyes and instantly knew she was aware of the entire journey I'd been on and that she'd taken some version of it herself.

I also knew that Virgie was a Firemaker, Peri was a Firemaker, and so was I. Sisters all.

"Yes, very powerful, Peri. *Pivotal* and powerful."

Then I remembered the two little tiles Peri had given me in the potting shed the day before.

Quickly I dug into my backpack, not quite certain what I would find. Inside, there was only one tile and sure enough, it was the one with the lotus and flame. I was not surprised. The tile with the candle in the cave was not mine, at least not now.

Maybe it would be later, or maybe never, but it didn't matter. I knew that I had chosen the perfect Seventh Door, and that soon Peri and I would cement the lotus and flame tile to the last altar in the garden.

I felt like laughing out loud with happiness but simply smiled and said. "Well, Peri, this was a much needed little bump on the head. This tile is the last one for the garden, if that's okay with you. I'm afraid I misplaced the other one."

"Misplaced, huh?" Peri chuckled. "Yes, this tile is perfect. Good choice, Helen. We'll put it up in the last altar as soon as you're feeling able. You sure you're all right?"

I smiled and nodded.

Then to the sun and the clouds, to Virgie and Peri and all the other Firemakers I'd met in my life without knowing it, I whispered, "I am The Firemaker, and I am finally, permanently, all right."

CHAPTER 32

PERSEPHONE'S JOURNEY

I spent that night at Peri's, and the next morning we went out to the garden and installed the last tile. It looked as if no other tile could ever have belonged there.

A little later, she drove me home with my bike in her trunk. Amazingly, the bike only had a few scrapes and wasn't going to need any work. After another day of resting at home I felt energized and called Peri to tell her I was coming over.

"You don't want me to come pick you up? I'd be happy to."

"Thanks, but no. I actually feel wonderful and I want to ride over."

"Okay, honey, but you be real careful."

"You can count on that. I'll see you in a few minutes."

When I arrived and knocked, Peri opened the door, and after the cats and birds noisily rearranged themselves here and there as usual, she reached into her shirt pocket and handed me a sticky note.

"Here, I forgot to give you this the other day. As I was walking into the hospital, that nice young EMT man, Eric, gave me this for you." She smiled, "Said to give him a call when you're feeling better if you have a mind to, and I imagine you have a mind to, right?"

I smiled and nodded. "Yeah, I think I have a mind to, lump on the head and all."

Peri fixed some tea and we sat silently in the living room for perhaps ten minutes, then I asked, "Is that how it was for you, Peri? Behind the Doors, I mean?"

She chuckled. "You mean does *every* Firemaker get started on the journey through the Land Behind the Doors by getting knocked unconscious riding a yellow bicycle?"

I rubbed the bump on my head and laughed, "No. I mean, how did you get to the Land Behind the Doors? How did you become a Firemaker?"

Her face became thoughtful and I could see she was remembering an old and beloved story. "Oh, it was nothing like the way you entered. There are a million ways the journey can start. I did it through meditation and guided visualization, even though I'd never meditated for one second when I started and certainly had never been aware of being guided toward anything by anyone.

"As I told you, after my Ed died and all my affairs were settled, I arranged for someone to look after the animals, locked up the garden, and went abroad to find my way again.

"Our mortgage insurance paid off the house. And I knew if I was careful and invested conservatively,

Ed's life insurance would be enough for me to do what I wanted. So off I went.

"I spent some time in Europe, then made my way on over into Africa and the Middle East with no idea where I was going, or even why, really.

"Eventually, I answered an ad placed by a university professor in Cairo and ended up working on some archaeological digs in the Valley of the Kings in Egypt for a while. It was slow, methodical work, not unlike gardening, so it was perfect for me.

"And, fortunately, the tasks I was hired to do didn't require any knowledge of archaeology, just attention to detail and patience. By then, I sure had plenty of all that.

"Anyway, after the dig was over, I decided to see more of Egypt and I met a woman on a rickety old steamboat going up the Nile.

"The encounter was similar in many ways to the day you came to me. I was just going *anywhere* that was away from the sadness of my recent past. But that was good enough to put me where I *needed* to be. We both know now that it was The City of Joy I was after.

"This woman was just waiting for me when I got on, is all I can say. Twenty seconds after I walked on board she just grabbed me by the arm and took charge. Don't misunderstand. She did it quite pleasantly. But it wasn't like I had any more choice about it than you did when Virgie sent you to me."

I smiled at the memory of the rain, my soggy hair, the collapsed paper bag and being rescued by dear Virgie. It seemed as if I'd eaten that banana light years ago, as if it was something that had happened to someone else in a distant galaxy.

Peri continued, "So, off and on for three days, she helped me attain a kind of trance state, sometimes in her stateroom, sometimes on deck under the stars in the wee hours of the morning when no other passengers were around.

"I went through seven doors, the same as you. But the *nature* of the seven doors I encountered was slightly different. While the essence of the lessons was exactly the same, they were geared to me specifically and to my level of understanding.

"I don't know what you saw, and it would be difficult to tell you what I saw. Remember this when your first novice finds you, as you found me. Her doors are not your doors or my doors. And even if you and she, or you and I, had both passed through the same door at the same time, the *way* the lessons were presented to us would still be different."

"Yes, I understand. Somehow I knew that."

Peri smiled, patted my hand, and rubbed me on the back as we stepped though her front door. "Of course you did, Helen. You're a Firemaker now."

We sat in silent companionship sipping our tea for nearly an hour as we'd done so many times before. Time was nothing to us, and her old house and the garden were the whole world right then.

When we finished, we walked our china to the kitchen. Peri took my cup and saucer and said, "Here, honey, let me take care of those. You go on home now. You don't want to overdo it. We'll pick up in the garden in the morning. Sure I can't give you a lift?"

I hugged her and said, "No, thank you, Peri. The ride over was good for me, but starting on the garden tomorrow sounds right. I still have a lot to absorb, and I'm ready for a hot shower and a nap. But there are two more things I need to ask you."

"Okay, honey, shoot."

"First, was there another door on your journey? I don't need the details but I just want to know if there were *two* doors to choose from at the end. Is that something you can tell me?"

Peri nodded and said, "Uh-huh. There was another door on my journey, too."

"Wow, so that's universal to the journey, too. Fascinating. I wonder what was behind the door I *didn't* choose?"

Peri just smiled knowingly. "I'm pretty sure you'll find that out eventually, Helen."

I waited, hoping she'd say more, but she didn't.

"And what was your other question, dear?"

"It's about your name, Persephone. I know you prefer Peri and that your name is a mouthful and all of that, but...well, there's more to it than that isn't there?"

Peri smiled and patted my arm. "Yes, child, there is. If I remember correctly you're not very familiar with the myth of Persephone?"

"I know virtually nothing about it, Peri, I'm embarrassed to say."

"Oh, there's nothing to be embarrassed about. The thing about myths is that the art is in the telling. And the myth of Persephone, like most *really* good stories, has more than one way of being told. But I'm a gardener, not a storyteller, so I'll do my best to give you the essence of it, at least as I know it.

"In Greek mythology, Persephone was the daughter of Zeus and Demeter. Her story begins on a lovely warm afternoon in a beautiful meadow filled with flowers of every sort and fragrance.

"Persephone was very beautiful and many men desired her. Hades, the god of the underworld, was one of those who coveted her. But Hades knew that Demeter would never consent to such a marriage for her daughter, so he plotted and he waited.

"When his chance came, he seized the moment, burst forth from the underworld through a mighty chasm in the ground, and abducted the maiden while she was gathering flowers.

"As you might imagine, Demeter was inconsolable over the disappearance of her daughter and when she figured out where she had been taken and by whom, she sent Hermes to the underworld to free her.

"As a goddess, Demeter's dominion was over plants and grains and growing things upon the earth. With her daughter gone, her great suffering caused Demeter to neglect her duties. Soon the fields and fruits, and the animals that fed on them, began to wither and die.

"When Hermes came for Persephone, Hades knew that Persephone was terribly lonely for her mother and the outside world and would never consent to stay with him on her own, so he devised a clever trap.

"When he released her to Hermes, he gave her several pomegranate seeds to eat on the journey home.

"Unfortunately for Persephone, the pomegranate seeds were enchanted, and once she swallowed them, she was doomed to return to Hades and the underworld for part of the year, every year.

"This curse was to last throughout all of time. So every year when the day approaches for Persephone to return to the underworld, Demeter's grief is so consuming that all growth stops on the surface of the world. That dormant period is called winter.

"But there is hope. At the end of Persephone's forced stay with Hades, she returns to her mother and life comes back to the earth and spring and the cycle of seasons begins again."

"What an interesting way to explain the seasons."

"Yes, it is. But it's more, too, Helen. Persephone's struggle between the world of light and the world of darkness is not unlike what you were told by The Firemaker about the dark, narrow cave.

"Virtually all human beings who exist on the Earth plane at any given time are some version of Persephone, constantly moving between periods of growth, light and joy, and periods of darkness and stasis.

"And even though we *prefer* the periods of light and obvious growth because they feel so wonderful, the times spent in stillness — in the darkness — are invaluable preparation times and opportunities for inner journeys.

"When we find ourselves apart from the light and then are returned to it, we see so much more clearly and appreciate everything so much more. Without those periods of contrast, we wouldn't choose to grow at all.

"We'd all just romp around the meadow like newborn calves, and that's fine for a while. That's what childhood is for, but it won't sustain and fulfill us over the long run.

"That's why my mother insisted that I be named Persephone and taught me about this myth, so that I would never forget that even the dark times are important and necessary.

"At some point, we will all reach the stage of growth that The Firemaker mentioned, the Unified Spirit. Then, the cycles of light and dark are not automatic any more, and we can choose for ourselves how we will grow and in what direction. Do you see?"

"Yes, Peri, I do. Your mother was a very wise woman and your name, Persephone, is beautiful, just like you. Thank you for sharing all this with me."

We walked out onto the front porch and I stepped down and straddled my bike. "Thank you for everything, Peri. I can't think of anything else to say because there aren't enough words. But you know how deeply I mean it, right?"

"I know, dear. And you're welcome. Someone did it for me, and someday you'll do it for someone, too."

I smiled at that because I knew she was right. Back when I had used the ring to focus on my career as The Firemaker guided me, I had seen that I was going back to school.

I would write and paint and I knew that I would teach, too. I would use my life and experience behind the Doors to create things that speak intimately to the heart. I would help others to find the City of Joy inside them, just as I had been helped.

Peri winked at me as if she knew my thoughts, and then reached into the pocket of her jacket. She pulled out a little navy blue book with gold lettering on the cover and handed it to me. There was a bright red ribbon around it, tied in a bow.

"When you find the time and things have settled down a bit, you'll want to read this. It belongs to you now.

"Run along before it starts to rain again. And watch those brakes on the other side of that hill. Goodbye for tonight my dear little Firemaker. I'll see you here tomorrow."

I smiled and nodded, accepted the book, and slipped it into my backpack without reading the cover, somehow knowing that was the proper way to do it.

"Thank you again, Peri. I'll see you tomorrow."

At home, I let the book sit in my backpack for the rest of the day and contented myself with experiencing this whole new way of being. I was happy and calm in a way I'd never, ever been. Everything was in alignment and I was whole.

Before my journey, I'd thought of my future as something created entirely out of the past. If you'd asked me how I viewed it, I'd have said it looked like a long, dark road of mind-numbing work and perpetually delayed fulfillment.

But life looked different now; it looked flexible and forgiving. There was time to grow and loads of resources built right inside of me to help me get to where I wanted to be.

The goals born of my Downstream Dream were coming closer to me as I was moving with Life's flow toward them. Believing that, knowing I was becoming what I sought to be, what I held outside myself as successful, worthy and whole inside, gave me a feeling of release.

If I kept moving forward, following my inner compass, I *would* live out the wonderful Possible Futures I glimpsed in the Pool. The visions I had seen there were as clear and bright to me as the debris in the Swamp of the Past had been murky and dark.

Living each day as merely another step in an interminable forced march that began with my birth had doomed me to years of regret, loneliness, and fear. But I'd had enough of that now.

The movement of life is *toward* us, not away. The beginning and the ending exist on a continuum that can only be fully understood from a larger perspective. Now that I had that, everything was changed.

Life seems as opposite from what I once believed about the way it worked as anything could be. Yet nothing outside me was different. The world still spins on its axis and orbits the sun. Earth is still a beautiful blue sphere revolving in a sea that is vast beyond measure.

Only I am different. *I am different.* I belong in the world, and I am not alone. The Universe has a place for me. It isn't for me to figure it all out; it's for me to open myself to what lies ahead, to listen to and bring forth what lives within. It's for me to make new fires that bring light and warmth and safety into the world from the sparks of my little piece of the sun.

This is what I was born to do.

CHAPTER 33

THE LITTLE BLUE BOOK

After dinner that night, I pulled out the little blue book that Peri had given me and untied the red ribbon. On the cover the title was written in fancy gold script. I opened it and read…

The Legacy of The Firemaker

Throughout all of human history there have been a rare and precious few who are called Firemaker.

It is they who bring the new into the old and help expand human potential in the world.

It is they who accomplish great things and lead humanity toward soaring new vistas filled with astounding Possible Futures.

They lead the world out of seemingly impossible dilemmas that, if left to unfold unchecked, would dash all hope and snuff out the warming fires of joy and compassion forever.

The names of those Firemakers are known to many.

But there are also many Firemakers who are ordinary in appearance and work quietly and without fanfare, doing extraordinary things that are vital to human survival.

Their deeds often go unnoticed and unheralded, and their names are not recorded in the books of history.

It matters not whether individual Firemakers are visible or unnoticed, or how their work is done.

They are nonetheless the creators of The Flame of Truth and agents of growth and change for the betterment for all.

...it of the rest of humanity?

...ork that is done by the masses of people is born out of ... ideas, discoveries and efforts of Firemakers — all of it.

Once a Firemaker ignites The Flame of Truth, others associate themselves with the new light and heat, using those elements to produce valuable and needed things.

These people are The Flamekeepers.

Most people in the world are Flamekeepers. They do not invent new ideas or discover new cures, but they apply the knowledge brought into the world by the Firemakers.

The differences between Firemakers and Flamekeepers are not so dramatic as they might seem.

Everyone has the potential to become a Firemaker, to carry that inner spark from place to place in their lives, lighting up the world wherever they go, whatever they do.

Most people secretly feel that potential, that special thing waiting just beyond their present understanding. They long for this something that they cannot name, often mistakenly looking outside at the world instead of inside themselves.

Most will never do the searching and work necessary to discover and use the Inner Flame. And so the world is filled with people standing next to the warming fires created by a very special few.

This is neither bad nor good. At this stage of human evolution, it is simply the way of things.

The general belief of humankind is that people must stay in place, tethered to whatever fire they find themselves beside at birth. It could be the fire of the birth family, town, country or traditions in which they were raised.

This is what most people do. They avoid the pain of uncertainty and turn away from the risk of adventure, never daring to imagine that they could travel elsewhere and make their own fire whenever necessary.

Thus, this is the fate of most human beings, and while it seems as if set in stone by outside forces or immutable societal laws, in truth it is most often self-imposed.

A Firemaker is a person with a piece of the sun that never goes out and who, from that, makes magical sparks.

A Firemaker can generate the Fire of Truth anywhere, and under any conditions, giving out warmth and light, and then step back and allow others to choose for themselves if they will embrace it.

A Firemaker does not judge others or their actions, but simply brings forth fire and lets others choose to use it or not.

And you may ask, "With the Firemakers here to show truth and create good, why is there so much madness and sorrow in the world?"

The answer is twofold: first, nothing but Cosmic Order usurps Free Will, even when it is used for destruction and *chaos. And Cosmic Order includes allowing Free Will in many situations, much of the time.*

Second, all illness comes from a broken heart.

To intentionally do harm is an act that spins out from an illness of the mind. And that illness only exists because the heart of that person, or someone close to that person, has been broken. No matter how evil the doer may seem, at the center is a broken heart.

That reality, expanded to extremes, creates the third group of powerful and destructive human beings, those who will not do the work of creating or tending the Fire of Truth, yet crave the power of fire all the same.

These people are called Shadowmakers.

The way of the Shadowmakers is to dash out of the darkness, steal a small burning branch from a fire created by others, and then run away with it into the night.

The horrible despots of history are Shadowmakers. They have plundered enough fuel to ignite raging wildfires of destruction across much of the world.

Shadowmakers create nothing that lasts; they merely steal fire and then pollute its beauty, trample on its Truth and damage the fragile balance of the Earth.

The least powerful in this group, the lost and the desperate, are unable to live without such things as too much strong drink, dark potions and dangerous pursuits, and eventually find no additional fuel.

As their stolen branches burn out, they are swallowed up by the darkness.

Shadowmakers are little more than social arsonists who stumble upon an opportune place and time to do their dreadful work and focus their Free Will on dark outcomes. This is where the evil things in the world issue forth, from people who spread stolen fire without understanding its source or true nature.

Shadowmakers have no knowledge of the origins and alchemy of fire, and so they do not recognize when combustion is nearing critical levels, or where it is safe to build a fire and where it is not.

A Firemaker, however, is the practitioner of an ancient art who conscientiously observes and builds and is devoted to warmth and light. A Firemaker can tell balance from imbalance, and recognize which Self, the Greater or Lesser, is acting.

A Firemaker comes into being as a result of much slow, methodical work. This is a process of winnowing away the negative and illuminating what is good in human beings, then connecting the good to all that individuals have the potential to be.

Brave adventurer, you have been led to this moment by other Firemakers and your Greater Self and are, at last, free to pursue the path of becoming a Unified Spirit.

You are a Firemaker now, and whenever you need guidance or strength, simply say these words, then be still and wait for the answers you seek, for they will come.

Say…

I AM THE FIREMAKER

And it is so.

Note:

The following page of chapter headings is included to facilitate this book's use in Dr. Marina R. Walker's teaching and training practice, and as a reference for the reader

Publisher, OakStar Press

SEVEN DOORS OF THE FIREMAKER

CHAPTER HEADINGS

SEVEN DOORS OF THE FIREMAKER

For further information about Dr. Walker's writing, teaching or workshops please visit her Web site at:

www.FiremakerInstitute.com

SEVEN DOORS OF THE FIREMAKER